Syntax of -ing Forms in Legal English

European University Studies

Europäische Hochschulschriften
Publications Universitaires Européennes

Series XIV
Anglo-Saxon Language and Literature

Reihe XIV Série XIV
Angelsächsische Sprache und Literatur
Langue et littérature anglo-saxonnes

Vol./Bd. 439

PETER LANG
Frankfurt am Main · Berlin · Bern · Bruxelles · New York · Oxford · Wien

Slávka Janigová

Syntax of -ing Forms in Legal English

PETER LANG
Internationaler Verlag der Wissenschaften

Bibliographic Information published by the Deutsche Nationalbibliothek
The Deutsche Nationalbibliothek lists this publication in the Deutsche Nationalbibliografie; detailed bibliographic data is available in the internet at <http://www.d-nb.de>.

Printed with financial support
of the University of Košice

ISSN 0721-3387
ISBN 978-3-631-57470-6

© Peter Lang GmbH
Internationaler Verlag der Wissenschaften
Frankfurt am Main 2008

www.peterlang.de

TABLE OF CONTENTS

LIST OF ABBREVIATIONS

–	functioning
Adj	adjective
Adv	adverbial
Adv of accomp/time	adverbial of accompanying circumstances/time
Aux	auxiliary
AP	Acts of Parliament
C_s	subject complement
C_o	object complement
CHD	Chancery Division, Law Reports
Conj	conjunction
DN	deverbal noun
FD	Family Division, Law Reports
FLA	Family Law Act
G	gerund
Inf	infinitive
LR	Law Reports
NP	noun phrase
O_D	direct object
O_{Prep}	prepositional object
Part	participle
Postmod	postmodifier
Premod	premodifier
Prep	preposition
PrepComp	prepositional complementation
PrepP	prepositional phrase
$PrepC_S$	prepositional subject complement
$PrepC_O$	prepositional object complement
S	subject
SemiCl	semi-clause construction
VN	verbal noun
TA	Theft Act

INTRODUCTION

The submitted study is concerned with *-ing* nominalisations in legal English. Western linguistics employs the term *'nominalisation'* to refer to the process of conveying a verb-related meaning by a noun phrase whose underlying structure is clausal and also to the constructions which result from this process. The Prague School tradition operates with the terms *'condensation/condensers'* and *'semi-clause constructions'*. The former is used to point to the fact that these forms enable the construction to dispense with explicit clausal structure which makes it more compact/condense while the latter refers to the structural character of these constructions that represents a transitional stage between a phrase and a clause due to the mixture of nominal and verbal features of their main component, accompanied with its verb-like semantics.

The following constructions are normally ranked with nominalisations:

(1) She was surprised *that he should pay her so much attention.* (Colen, 1984:16)

(2) She did not know *where to go.* (Colen, 1984:16)

(3) *To refuse the offer* would be a mistake. (Colen, 1984:16)

(4) He hated *attending wedding receptions*. (Colen, 1984:16)

(5) *His denying of the charge* only made matters worse. (Colen, 1984:16)

(6) *His denial of the charge* was not accepted. (Colen, 1984:16)

Our research is aimed to study the types represented by exx (4) (*gerunds, participles*) and (5) (*-ing verbal nouns*) and marginally, for the sake of comparison, also ex 6 (*non-ing verbal nouns*). We intend to provide the account of their actual occurrence in the selected corpus in respective syntactic functions in order to be able to summarise the factors that influence the choice of a particular type within a verb-related semantic range that unites them. We adopt the method of descriptivist grammarians proceeding from the detection of actual corpus occurrence of the examined constructions, followed by the interpretation of the outcome of the syntactic analysis, proceeding towards linguistic generalisation as to the above-mentioned conditioning factors.

We consider structural functionalism of the Prague School as inherent grounds of our approach as the function of the *-ing* form in a construction of which it is the main element as well as the function of the whole construction headed by the *-ing* element on the immediately higher syntactic level in a particular context is the primary criterion for distinguishing respective types of *-ing* forms.

The study is composed of the following parts:

Chapter One – is aimed to summarise our approach to *-ing* forms presented as a cline or graded scale model. The phenomenon of *-ing* forms allows for demonstration of the impact of the syntactic function of a linguistic unit on its form in the course of time. This impact will be considered in terms of transitionality or gradience, the principle present in all of the examined aspects (semantic, structural, syntactic and also as regards the process of formation of these forms and inflectional *versus* derivational status if the *-ing* ending). Discussion is conceptually centred around the word-class assignment in relation to respective types of *-ing* forms, which inevitably depends on considering the above-mentioned aspects.

We attempt to defend the conception that the verb-related meaning expressed by the *-ing* forms represents a scalar semantic spectre the members of which convey different degrees or combinations of processuality, factuality and conceptuality. This conception underlines our examination of the morphological and syntactic potential of respective realisations of *-ing* forms and also the specific interpretation of the structural status of constructions headed by the same (phrase – semi-clause construction – clause).

As the shift in the syntactic interpretation may only be observed in the projection of time it seemed quite useful to employ also a diachronic approach. Hence we provide a brief diachronic account of the origination, development and syntactic specification of the *-ing* forms. The conclusions arrived at in the end of Chapter One, thus, result from a combination of both the diachronic and synchronic approaches.

Chapter Two – contains the characteristics of the corpus that is to be subject to structural/syntactic analysis. We also outline theoretical approaches to the terms legal language, language of the law and stylistic stratification of legal discourse. The chapter further describes the method of analysing and examples of the syntactic analysis itself, arranged according to respective syntactic functions performed by verbal nouns, gerunds and participles in order of their occurrence in the corpus consisting of Law Reports and Acts of Parliaments.

Chapter Three – consists of tabulation of data based on the corpus research (Law Reports) and their interpretation. The frequency data concern the total occurrence of all *-ing* forms in the text as assigned to particular word classes, total occurrence of sentence condensers in respective syntactic functions, occurrence of gerundial and participial morphological forms, occurrence and forms of the agent expressed explicitly with gerundial and participial constructions, including findings concerning the occurrence of absolute and dangling gerundial and participial constructions.

We point to the relevance of making distinction between respective types of *-ing* forms by reference to their specific semantic, structural and syntactic potential. We demonstrate it on the examples which show only seemingly similar patterning of certain structures and provide tests that may be helpful in selecting the appropriate option of syntactic interpretation.

Chapter Four – this part is aimed at comparing results of the syntactic analyses of both parts of our corpus in terms specified in the outline of Chapter Three hereinabove.

To test whether the stylistic factor may be included in the list of factors influencing the choice of an *-ing* type we attempted to set out, tentantively, a working hypothesis that may be subject to verification in the course of our present research and that shall be commented on in the fourth chapter of our study:

When comparing the ratio of occurrences of the respective types of *-ing* forms in two stylistic layers of legal English (namely the legislation and judgments) we expect the outcome of the research to show that the genre of Acts of Parliament is more nominal than that of judicial decisions. The style of judgments seems to be less rigid, normative and formulaic in character than that of legislative enactments. We expect this to be proved by:

- higher number of participial occurrence;
- lower ratio of verbal noun *vs* gerundial occurrence;
- lower occurrence of *-ing* forms as complements of prepositions;

in the sample texts of Law Reports than the distribution of the respective forms in the Acts of Parliament.

This hypothesis may be supported methodologically by Quirk's comments concerning the relevance of the comparative corpus frequency data for the possibility of treating the stylistic element as a conditioning factor in respect of the occurrence of a certain language phenomenon: "What we may expect from it is objective evidence for the description of one aspect of grammatical structure in the works we have discussed and for the statement of the frequency of particular variants in individual texts as well as in the corpus as a whole. Moreover, the method allows us to study the role of conditioning factors in the selection of variants." (Quirk, 1995:111)

Conclusion – summarises the conditioning factors which play a role in the selection of a particular type of condensers.

CHAPTER ONE

1. Hierarchy of criteria

The impetus instigating our interest in the issue of the English *-ing* forms was rather practical. We were, of course, aware of their existence and of the most important morpho-syntactic features of their particular realisations, nevertheless, the rules governing the choice of a certain form did not seem quite definite. Our first attempts to approach the issue of the English *-ing* forms were connected with a great deal of confusion and uncertainty caused by terminological discrepancies that we encountered while consulting the current linguistic works, studies and articles dealing with the subject-matter in question. Hence, we started with identification of terminology and delimitation of several groups or classes of *-ing* forms sharing similar qualities. As far as the terminology concerns, the authors handling the matter of *-ing* forms can be basically divided into two groups: those who prefer labelling distinct types separately and those who use a uniform label '*-ing* forms' for all of them. Discrepancies also exist in the latter group as different labels are attached to the same forms by different authors.

To demonstrate the variety of *-ing* forms we provide the following examples including non-*ing* deverbal and verbal nouns which belong to our concept of the verb-related semantic scalar spectre :

(1) The manager is authorised to bind the company with his sole **signature**. (private instrument)

(2) *There is no statutory prohibition against* ***hearings*** *in chambers in the family cases.* (FD)

(3) *... total number of* ***signatures*** *not followed by ratifications:16; ...* (Chromá, 2003:443)

(4) *Slightly more that 5000 boats were registered with the Coast Guard prior to the recent* ***passage*** *of the state boating law.* (Brown Corpus 1979)

(5) *If after the* ***making*** *of a divorce order or the grant of a decree annulling a marriage either spouse remarries, that spouse is not entitled to apply...* (FLA)

(6) *The Manager's appointment shall commence upon the* ***signing*** *of this agreement.* (private instrument)

(7) *In Britain this entails the* ***passing*** *of the statute through both Houses of Parliament and its receiving the royal assent in the required manner.* (Kurzon, 1986:14)

(8) *With the* ***uttering*** *of the sentence 'I take thee.' the marriage is felicitously performed provided that other conditions are fulfilled, ...* (Kurzon, 1986:43)

(9) *The United States, which has signalled its intention to ratify by formally* ***signing*** *the Convention, now stands as the only industrialized country in the world and one of only two United Nations member states yet to make this legal commitment to children.* (Chromá, 2003:443)

(10) *In 1914, at the outbreak of he First World War, the Speaker of the House of Commons ruled that there was no need to suspend standing orders to accelerate the procedure of* ***passing*** *several emergency statutes, since Parliament had the right to enact a statute in any way it thinks fit.* (Kurzon, 1986:15)

(11) *Except as herein provided no Member shall be separately compensated on a salaried basis for service performed in* ***carrying out*** *the operation of the Company, ...* (private instrument)

(12) *The accountant may be removed by the Manager without* ***assigning*** *any cause.* (private instrument)

(13) *The Company shall maintain such accounting records as the Members, or* ***failing*** *any direction from them, the Manager may deem fit.* (private instrument)

(14) *If the applicant is not in occupation, an order under this section must contain provision* ***giving*** *the applicant the right to enter...* (FLA)

(15) *... that the trustees and managers of that other scheme are able and* ***willing*** *to accept such payment and create those rights.* (FLA)

(16) *... a spouse's matrimonial home rights are not an* ***overriding*** *interest within the* ***meaning*** *of that Act...* (FLA)

(17) *The undersigned owners agree to share in all post formation capital contribution, profits and surplus of the Company* ***according to*** *the percentage of their ownership.* (private instrument)

(18) ***During** the course of the term for which this Company is formed, the Company shall carry liability insurance in such amounts as are deemed appropriate by the Members.* (private instrument)

(19) ***Notwithstanding** any enactment to the contrary, where property has been stolen or obtained by fraud or other wrongful means, the title to that or any other property shall not be affected by reason only of the conviction of the offender.* (TA)

(20) *The enactments mentioned in Schedule 3 to this Act... are hereby repealed to the extent specified in column 3 of that Schedule, and, **notwithstanding that** the foregoing sections of this Act do not extend to Scotland, ..., the Schedule shall have effect to repeal it...* (TA)

(21) *The question whether the provision of paragraphs... is to be determined **according as** those provisions have or have not already had effect in relation to the statutory tenancy.* (FLA)

(22) *... any child who is **living** with or might be reasonably expected to live with either party to the proceedings; ...* (FLA)

As can be seen from the above list, the first striking feature is the functional overload of one form. The question is arising whether what we are facing here are different syntactic functional employments of one lexeme or whether we have several separate lexemes or word forms. ("Lexemes can be regarded as groupings of one or more word forms, which are individuated by their roots and/or derivational affixes." (Cruse, 2004:86)) In this case, as shown above, the forms in question are differentiated neither by their roots, nor by their affixes (the derivational *versus* inflectional status of the *-ing* ending will be treated in section 4.3) The problem is thus necessarily associated with the word-class assignment of particular realisations of *-ing* forms.

The parts of speech classification derived from the Greek and Latin grammars is obviously based on three criteria:

1. semantic or notional (denotation of substance, actions/states or qualities)

2. morphological or formal or paradigmatic (capability of being subject to inflection)

3. syntactic or functional (the function of a particular unit in a sentence).

As far as the *-ing* forms is concerned, the above mentioned functional overload of one form is reflected in all of the three respects. As regards the semantic level, their representatives are capable of conveying substances, actions and qualities. The above examples demonstrate that some of the *-ing* forms function as autosemantic while others occur as synsemantic items. As for the syntactic factor, the *-ing* forms may function as subject, subject complement, verb element, attribute, object, adverbial as well as connectors on the phrasal and clausal level (prepositions and conjunctions). The morphological potential of a particular *-ing* form (expressed by morphological categories) depends exactly on its actual syntactic employment.

The feature of contextual dependence of English words has been frequently pointed out by numerous scholars: "A great many English words may, if considered isolatedly (as parts of 'language'), belong to more classes than one, but in each particular application (in 'speech') they can only belong to one, and it is generally easy to determine which one." (Jespersen, 1965g:41). This factor must be inevitably taken into consideration when attempting to determine the word-class assignment of a particular *-ing* form. It is only the actual contextual occurrence in a particular syntactic function which indicates its morpho-syntactical potential as well as its semantic range. While the assignment of certain *-ing* occurrences may be quite safe, the status of others may be less straightforward. Difficulties arise especially where the word-class status is to be assigned to an *-ing* form that is not considered as a fully-fledged representative of the recognised word classes or in the absence of necessary contextual indicators (*eg of*-postmodification *versus* object complementation, form of the agent, type of modifier).

Some authors defend the formal criteria as a means to distinguish different parts of speech, others underline the functional aspect as being crucial in the hierarchy of the above criteria – Tesniére (1934), similarly Ferenčík: "In fact it seems that the structural criterion, i.e. the positions of an element in the structural hierarchy, takes the upper hand over the other two criteria." (Ferenčík, 2002:18). Although defending the former approach, Jespersen admits that "... formal criteria are not always present with the same degree of clearness, and Modern English in many cases has obliterated distinctions that were formerly more evident". (Jespersen, 1965b:6).

The mixture of qualities, as presented above, led us to establish a hierarchy in respect of the criteria relevant to the word-class assignment. We decided to ground our approach on the **concept of function** as superordinate to the rest of the criteria and we attempted to identify the morphological and semantic potential of respective occurrences of *-ing* forms from the perspective of their function in a unit of the immediately higher linguistic level (phrase – clause – sentence). In respective syntactic functions the summary of morphological potential resulted in the separation of five groups (beside the adjective, prepositional and conjunctive status of some of the *-ing* representatives). We decided to attach distinct labels to the types of *-ing* forms which share common qualities from the semantic, morphological and syntactic point of view. This approach is derived from the Prague School tradition and it enables to simplify their treatment. With autosemantic word-classes the morpho-syntactic account is underlined by the position in the scalar semantic spectre of verb-related meaning that respective types occupy.

2. Degrees of nominalisation

2.1 Summary of the criteria for distinguishing degrees of nominalisation.

As the English linguists are not unified as far as the classification and terminology applicable to *-ing* forms concerns our starting point shall be the outline of the characteristics of respective types of *-ing* forms followed by the terminology that we have found in the works of prominent English linguists as well as the one that we have adopted in the present research. We have observed that all the authors examined concur in ascertaining degrees of nominal and verbal character which are manifested in the morphology and structure as well as the repertory of syntactic functions performed by the *-ing* forms. These degrees range from a pure nominal character through the mixture of nominal and verbal features to pure verbality.

The nominal character of *-ing* forms may be tested by the admissibility of :

a) plural inflection;
b) determiners: (*i*) indefinite article, (*ii*) definite article,
(*iii*) demonstrative pronouns, (*iv*) possessive case,
(*v*) indefinite pronouns;
c) adjective premodification;
d) postmodification by an *of*-construction;
e) occurrence after prepositions.

The verbal character of *-ing* forms may be tested by:

f) the agent expressed by the objective/common case;
g) preservation of verbal government;
h) tense, voice and aspect contrasts;
i) modification by an adverb;
j) occurrence after conjunctions.

We attempted to apply the above criteria to the following set of sentences taken from CGEL (1985:1291) and to tabulate the results as provided below.

(1) *The Manager is authorised to bind the company with his sole* ***signature***. (private instrument)

(2) ... *total number of* ***signatures*** *not followed by ratifications:16;* ... (Chromá, 2003:443)

(3) *However, even if a particular contract requires a writing, this does not mean that both parties must sign it or that the* ***signing*** *occurs at the time of contracting.* (Chromá, 2003:377)

(4) *The United States, which has signalled its intention to ratify by formally* ***signing*** *the Convention, now stands as the only industrialized country in the world and one of only two United Nations member states yet to make this legal commitment to children.* (Chromá, 2003:443)

(5) ***Having signed*** *the contract the party cannot revoke his/her offer without being subject to legal consequences.* (private instrument)

(6) *If there was an express agreement that the man who was* ***signing*** *was not to be liable, the section would not apply.* (Chartrand, 1997:92)

Table 1. Nominal *vs*. verbal properties of *-ing* forms.

	1	2	3	4	5	6
Plural form	+	+	–	–	–	–
A, an	+	+	–	–	–	–
The	+	+	+	–	–	–
This, that	+	+	+	–	–	–
Possessive case	+	+	+	+	–	–
No, any	+	+	+	+	–	–
Of-phrase	+	+	+	–	–	–
Adjective premod.	+	+	+	–	–	–
Introduced by a preposition	+	+	+	+	–	–
Introduced by a conjunction	–	–	–	–	+	+
Objective/common case	–	–	–	+	+	+
Adverbial modification	–	–	–	+	+	+
Object complementation	–	–	–	+	+	+
Voice contrast	–	–	–	+	+	+
Aspect contrast – progressive/nonprogresive	–	–	–	–	+	+
Aspect contrast – perfect/nonperfect	–	–	–	+	+	+
Tense contrast	–	–	–	–	–	+
No. of nominal features	9	9	7	3	0	0
No. of verbal features	0	0	0	5	7	8

2.2 Terminology applied to respective groups of *-ing* forms.

The above analysis resulted in the separation of five groups of *-ing* forms ranging from fully nominal forms (Groups 1 and 2), to fully verbal forms (Group 6) with three groups lying between these two extremes (in the sense of complete nominality or verbality), showing a mixture of nominal and verbal properties with the increasing degree of verbality and decreasing degree of nominality in the direction from Group 3 to Group 5.

There is a lot of discrepancies concerning the terminology relating to *-ing* forms used in selected linguistic references. Basically, various authors differ in one respect: some of them employ a *discrete* method of interpretation of the *-ing* forms distinguishing for example between *deverbal nouns*, *verbal nouns*, *gerunds* and *participles*, while others prefer putting all the *-ing* items under an umbrella term *-ing forms* without terminological differentiation (this may be referred to as a *gradient* mode of interpretation). Holders of both approaches attempt to justify their own positions by various reasons which shall be supplied along with the terminology employed. Terminological variants shall be tabulated in Table 2.

Jespersen, O. (1965, 1966)

The author distinguishes verbal elements which have the sentence-building power (called *finite verb forms*) and those that do not have it. The latter type is referred to as *verbids* (and they include participles and infinitives). In his notes on zero-derivation, Jespersen argues against the non-existence of separated parts of speech in English by pointing to the fact that the context always determinedly shows how a word should be functionally interpreted and this contextual determination is accompanied by the existence of formal distinctive criteria exemplified by a couple *love* (the noun with the plural *loves*) – *love* (the verb with the morphological forms of the 3rd person singular *loves*, *-d* preterite and participle and *-ing* participle and gerund). Hence *gerund* is for him a morphological form of a verb. One of the reasons why the gerund is treated like a verb is "evidently the formal identity with the first participle" (Jespersen, 1966:320). On the other hand, Jespersen also considers it as a special kind of nexus substantive which took over some syntactic characteristics of the verb which cannot be found in the rest of the nexus-substantives concluding finally that "it may therefore be termed a hybrid between these two word-classes, and as such has become an extremely supple means of combining and subordinating ideas." (Jespersen, 1966:320)

Jespersen's conception of the gerund, however, includes also the forms that may form a plural and take determination and of-postmodification (*ie* substantivised *-ing* forms), *eg:*

(7) *He imitated the putting of a noose about a man's throat.* (Jespersen, 1966:322 from Shakespeare)

Curme, G.O. (1980)

In his work *A Grammar of the English Language*, first published in 1935, Curme treats the participle and the gerund as infinite forms of the verb, along with the infinitive. What should distinguish them from the finite verbal forms is the fact that they do not have inflectional endings and so they are incapable of indicating their agreement with the subject. The author seems to be mixing terminology as in the following sentence: "The infinite forms have fewer tenses than finite verbs, but they express the time relations fairly well." (Curme, 1980a:203) We may deduce from it that these forms are intuitively placed outside the regular verbal paradigm. Participles and gerunds are further considered as lacking forms for mood and aspect (the progressive aspect may be expressed only in the perfect tense). They are restricted to subordinate clauses where they compete with finite forms from which they do not differ in respect of meaning, they only serve as their substitutes. "The finite forms can express finer shades of thought than the infinite forms as they are richer in means of expression, hence they must often be used; but the infinite forms are great favorites in practical life by reason of their handiness and are highly prized in choice language by reason of their elegant simplicity." (Curme, 1980a:204)

Curme finds it necessary to make a distinction between the gerund and the participle on account of their distinct functions (their formal identity is viewed as 'unfortunate'). "While the participle has the function and the position of an adjective, the gerund has the function and the position of a noun: '*Rearing* a large family is no easy task.' Here *rearing* has the full force of a verb, but at the same time it has the function of a noun, for it is the subject of the sentence." (Curme, 1980a:215)

Another principal feature that he associates with the gerund is that it serves as the object of a preposition, forming together a prepositional clause. This prepositional clause may modify a noun in which case it functions as an adjective element. In the cases where it modifies a verb, adjective , or participle its function may be interpreted as either "an object if its relation to the governing word is very close (exemplified in (8)), but it is an adverbial element if its relation to its governing word is less close (exemplified in (9))." (Curme, 1980a:215)

(8) *He insisted upon his wife's joining him in the deceit.* (Curme, 1980a:215)

(9) *He can't walk yet without my helping him.* (Curme, 1980a:215)

As for the origin of these forms Curme holds that the gerund developed from the Old English verbal noun ending in *-ung/-ing* belonging to the strong declension type *talu* with the exception of the drop of final *u*. In Middle English this form started to take an accusative object and in early Modern English it developed tense and voice forms. "Today, the verbal gerund is a very common construction, but in certain expressions older gerunds have been replaced by present participles." (Curme, 1980a:244 – 245)

As far as the terminology concerns Curme distinguishes between nominal and verbal gerund, the former allowing for *of*-postmodification and the latter following the valency pattern of the related verb.

Domestic scholarship deriving their conceptions from the tradition of Prague School tend to distinguish 'deverbal nouns, verbal nouns, gerunds and participles' and they employ the term 'semi-clause constructions' to denote the structural status of those termed gerunds and participles. The term 'semi-clause constructions' was first used by Vilém Mathesius, one of the founders and most influencing personalities of this School.

Mathesius, V., (1975)

Mathesius separates *-ing* forms termed *gerunds* from the category of *verbal nouns* when they display verbal features (taking the same object as the corresponding finite verb form, expressing voice and relatively also time distinctions). Basically, Mathesius treats the *gerund* as a special type of *verbal noun*. And he employs the term *participles* to refer to Group 5 and 6 *-ing* forms.

In his paper 'Řeč a sloh' (1966) Mathesius introduces the term *semi-clausal constructions,* which include the apposition and the transgressive (Mathesius, 1966:73). He characterises them as structures which have not acquired a status of sentence, but still cannot be considered as simple elements of a clause structure. This term has been adopted in the Czech English linguistics to refer to the structural status of Group III and IV *-ing* forms.

Trnka, B., (1956).

Trnka considers as the only justification for separating the categories of *-ing* forms, namely *participles* and *gerunds,* the efforts of traditional linguistics to find direct correspondence of English grammatical forms with those of Latin. He points out that what is denoted as the English *gerund* differs from the Latin *gerund* in that the former can express, to a certain extent, verbal tense and voice and can be determined by possessive pronouns or indefinite pronouns *no, any* even when it is used after prepositions and takes direct object, which he exemplifies as follows:

(10) *There is no denying the fact.* (Trnka,1956:106)

Trnka, however, is aware of the specific nominal construction of the *-ing* form when direct object is impossible and the preposition *of* is required after adnominal case, attributive adjective, articles or pronouns other than *no* and *any*:

(11) *in the making of anthology* (Trnka,1956:106)

(12) *in making anthology* (Trnka,1956:106)

(13) *this building of a house* (Trnka,1956:106)

(14) *this building a house* *. (Trnka,1956:106)

Direct object can be found in these constructions only in the Early Modern English, *eg:*

(15) *for the stealing sheep* (Trnka,1956:106)

whereas in present day English the only possible variants are :

(16) *for the stealing of sheep* (Trnka, 1956:106)

(17) *for stealing sheep* (Trnka, 1956:106).

Trnka maintains that the *-ing* form is a form unique to the English language which does not have counterparts in Latin or Czech. It is flexible in respect of expressing or suppressing verbal or nominal force of its potential in accordance with communicative goals with a possibility of combining its verbal and nominal features when necessary.

Vachek, J., (1961)
Similarly, J. Vachek finds it necessary to distinguish between the categories of *gerund* and *participle*, regardless of the identity of their forms and certain grammatical capabilities, due to the main factor which is the specific combination of verbo-nominal features in the category of *gerund*. Both of them (V. Mathesius and J. Vachek), however, admit that in some concrete instances (those with juxtaposition of the element operating as a subject of the construction – *apo koinu* structures) it is very difficult to decide on interpreting the form structurally as *gerundial* or *participial, eg*:

(18) *He would not hear of that being possible.* (Mathesius, 1975:151)

1. *(of that being possible)* – *prepositional* object realised by a semi-clause construction comprising the *-ing* form termed *gerund* with absolutely attached subject *that;*
2. *(that being possible)* – semi-clause construction comprising the *-ing* form ranked with participles postmodifying the object *that* of the finite verb in the matrix clause.

Dušková, L., (1988)
The author asserts that distinguishing between the *gerund* and *participle* is based on the syntactic operation of *-ing* forms classed under either of the headings, according to which the *gerund* belongs to the word class of nouns while the *participle* ranks with the adjectives. If *gerunds* or *participles* occur in the same syntactic function they are usually formally distinguished, *eg* a modifying *-ing* form has a specific intonation and stress pattern in accordance with either its *gerundial* or *participial* nature. This distinction is, moreover, supported by the difference in the semantics of the two kinds of premodifiers.

"An adverbial *-ing* form is indicated as *gerund* by being governed by a preposition, ..., as *participle* by being preceded by a conjunction." (Dušková, 1988:269, "Adverbiální *-ing*-ový tvar bývá indikován jako gerundium přítomností předložky, ..., participium přítomností spojky..." Transl. Janigová). The author admits that "Where the syntagmatic context of the *gerund* and the *participle* lacks differentiation and the sentence position admits both forms, the distinction between them is obliterated..." (Dušková, 1988:269, "Není-li syntagmatický kontext gerundia a participia odlišen a připouští-li větná pozice oba tvary, rozdíl mezi nimi se stírá..." Transl. Dušková).

The author uses the term *deverbal noun* (*deverbativní substantivum*) to denote both Group 1,2 and 3, *gerund* (*gerundium*) to cover Group 4, *participle* (participium) to term Group 5 and *participle as an element of a complex verb construction* (*participium jako součást složeného slovesného tvaru*) for Group 6 *-ing* forms.

Marková, M., (1986)
In her study on the occurrence of the *verbal noun* and the *gerund* in the syntactic function of object in selected texts, Marková comes to the conclusion that it is not always possible to draw a dividing line between 'the true *gerund*' and the constructions postmodified by an *of*-phrase. Rather than drawing sharp lines between them she describes them in terms of centre and periphery. The centre would then be constituted by the true *verbal gerund* (*ie gerund* with an object complement, the subject of gerundial action being expressed by the possessive or common case of a noun or a pronoun). Further from the centre there would be *-ing* forms with simultaneous verbal and nominal modifiers whose occurrence may be objectionable from the stylistic point of view (*eg* article plus direct

object) and even further, *gerunds* whose verbal features are reduced only to meaning (*ie verbal nouns* of action with an article and the preposition *of*). Also the low frequency of the *verbal noun* (the ratio of its frequency of occurrence in relation to the *gerund* is 1:20) points to the peripheral nature of such constructions.

Hais, K., (1991)

The author employs the following terminology:

- *verbal nouns* to denote Group I and II,
- *gerund* to refer to a form which is 'partly verbal and partly nominal' (Hais, 1991:273), here Group 4,
- *participle* which he ranks with 'nonfinite verb forms capable of expressing tense and voice' (Hais, 1991:262), here Group 5.

Kjellmer, G., (1980)

Kjellmer maintains that "a *gerund* is something of a taxonomic anomaly, standing astride, as it does, the boundary between nouns and verbs. It incorporates nominal and verbal characteristics simultaneously..." (Kjellmer, 1980:53). He also points to the analogy with the *gerund* in Latin as the English *gerund* is primarily non-modal *ie* "it does not add an element of possibility, impossibility, contingency or necessity to the basic meaning of the verb." (Kjellmer, 1980:47) He is also aware of the fact that in some circumstances the English *gerund* "acquires characteristics reminiscent of the Latin *gerundive*, the verbal adjective which normally has a prominent modal semantic component and which can be used predicatively like a noun." (Kjellmer, 1980:47)

Kjellmer refers to both the *-ing* forms in the sentences:

(19) *Writing a book is no easy matter.* (Kjellmer, 1980:54), and

(20) *The writing of a book is no easy matter.* (Kjellmer, 1980:54)

as *gerunds,* but he admits that the *-ing* in (19) is more verbal than in (20). He analyses these constructions in relation to modality to support especially the hypothesis of his in which he stipulates that there is "a tendency for *gerunds* with primarily nominal characteristics to have non-modal interpretations" and for those "with primarily verbal characteristics to have modal interpretations." (Kjellmer, 1980:54)

We may thus conclude that he terms Groups 3 and 4 *-ing* forms as *gerunds*, although in his study there is no reference to Group 5 *-ing* forms.

Lees, R. B., (1960)
In his paper *The Grammar of English Nominalizations,* published in 1960, R.B. defines the concept of *nominalisation* as a specific term to serve for the transformationalist linguistic description. Lees views *nominalisations* as transforms of underlying embedded sentences whose constituents mirror the internal structure of the sentence from which they are derived. "When we examine the internal structure of more complex *nominals* we see that it usually incorporates the major grammatical relations found in whole sentences. That is, within the complex subject of a sentence, for example, we might find the transformed subject, verb, object of an underlying sentence." (Lees, 1960:XVIII) He transformationally describes the *nominalisation* process in the following way: "In the usual case the transformation serves to generate from one of the two source-sentences which we might call the 'constituent-sentence', a certain transform, say a nominal, and then from the other, termed the 'matrix-sentence', it generates a new string with the transform of the constituent-sentence substituted in for some predecessor constituent of the matrix-sentence." (Lees, 1960:55) "The nominals generated by the (nominalization rules) are not themselves sentences, but rather they are noun-like versions of sentences. (Lees, 1960:54)" What *nominalisations* have in common with nouns is their nominal function within the sentence (complementation of verbs, adjectives, nouns and prepositions performing the functions of subject, object /direct, indirect, prepositional/, subject and object complements). The following structures have been described as *nominalisations* (the list is not complete):

Factive nominal
that-clauses

(21) I told her *that he saw us.* (Lees, 1960:60)

wh-clauses

(22) I know *what he did.* (Lees, 1960:59)

Infinitival nominal

(23) *I force him to go.* (Lees, 1960:74)

Action nominal (1st nominal)

(24) *His drawing* fascinated me because he always did it left handed. (*his rapid drawing of the picture*) (Lees, 1960:64)

Agentive nominal

(25) *He is the cooker of the meat.* (Lees,1960:69)

(26) *He is the stealer of the money.* (Lees, 1960:69)

Gerundive nominal (2nd nominal)

(27) *His eating vegetables* is surprising. (Lees, 1960:71)

Derived verbal

(28) *His denial of the charge* was not accepted.

For our present study dealing with *-ing nominalisations* we should like to point to the following relevant notes from Lees's work. The author exemplifies three types of *-ing* forms (he uses the expression '*gerund*' as an umbrella term):

(29) *I approved of his writing because he was better at it than the others.* (Lees, 1960:64)

(30) *I approved of his writing because they hadn't heard from him for so long.* (Lees, 1960:64)

(31) *I approved of his writing because it was so legible.* (Lees, 1960:64)

He terms the *-ing* forms in the above examples the *1st*, *2nd* and *3rd nominal* respectively. The *3rd nominal* is, according to him, normally a concrete noun (count or, in this case, a mass noun). Lees distinguishes it strictly from the *nominalisations* which are abstract and have an underlying sentence structure (*ie* the *1st* and *2nd nominals*). The *1st* and *2nd nominals*, though being homomorphic, stand in sharp semantic contrast: the *1st nominal* refers to an action, a way of doing, while the second refers to a fact. Lees points to the fact that "non-action verbs in general seem not have any *1st nominal* at all, *eg:*

(32) **His having of a hat...*

(33) * *His resembling of his mother...*

but all verbs have *2nd nominals*, *eg*:

(34) *His having a hat...*

(35) *His resembling his mother...*" (Lees, 1960:66)

"Parallel to the *1st nominal* there is for many verbs another in which the nominal head is a *derived verbal.*" (Lees, 1960:66)

Chomsky, N., (1970)

10 years later N. Chomsky in his work *Remarks On Nominalizations* analyses three types of nominalisations, namely *gerundive nominals*, *derived nominals* and so called '*mixed forms*'. The first term corresponds to what in the Prague School is termed *gerund*, the second is a terminological counterpart of '*deverbal noun*' denoting a noun expressing verbal action as a nominal concept and the last one to the term '*verbal noun*' which may be exemplified as follows:

(36) *John's refusing the offer* (Chomsky, 1970:215) – *gerundive nominals*

(37) *John's refusal of the offer* (Chomsky, 1970:215) – *derived nominals*

(38) *John's refusing of the offer* (Chomsky, 1970:215) – *mixed forms*

In his treatise Chomsky contends that Lees's transformational rules which account for the existence of various kinds of nominalisations are not unexceptional and that there is a multitude of syntactic and semantic differences between nominalisations and sentences. He calls his approach 'lexicalist' as opposed to Lees's 'transformationalist'. He deals with irregularities which exist in the relation of *derived nominals* to their presumed source sentence in respect of syntactic as well as semantic features.

Chomsky basically concurs with Lees in respect of *gerundive nominals,* admitting that they are a rather regular grammatical transforms of underlying sentence-like propositions of subject-predicate form. Their internal structure is therefore inherently clausal. According to him, *gerundive nominals* "can be formed fairly freely from propositions of subject-predicate form, and relation of meaning between the nominal and the propositions is quite regular. Furthermore the nominal does not have the internal structure of a noun phrase; thus we cannot replace *John's* by any determiner *(eg: that, the),* nor can we insert adjectives into gerundive nominal." (Chomsky, 1970:187).

Inherent structure of *derived nominals* is, on the contrary, phrasal. In the formation of *derived nominals*, however, the semantic considerations (which are quite varied and idiosyncratic) interfere with regularity of transformational rules. Chomsky contends that in this respect *gerundive nominals* are much more productive.

He refers to the third type as having some peculiar properties. Like *derived nominals* they "appear to have the internal structure of noun phrases;

thus the possessive subject can be replaced by a determiner. On the other hand, adjective insertion seems quite unnatural in this construction." (Chomsky, 1970:214). Chomsky maintains that this construction is of limited productivity and that it is "rather clumsy, though quite comprehensible, when a *derived nominal* also exists." (Chomsky, 1970:215) The third type thus combines a phrase-like form with verbal semantics. Chomsky treats it as the least productive type giving way to the *derived nominals*.

Quirk, R., *et al.*,(1985)

The Chomsky's lexicalist position as opposed to the Lees' transformationalist approach is also defended by Quirk *et al.* (1995:95) who refuses strict transformationalist analogies between action nominalisations and underlying sentences (*'the consideration of N'* transformed as *'(M) considered N'* is not equivalent to *'the picture of N'* to be transformed as *'(M) painted N'*).

Quirk *et al.* stress the gradience from *deverbal nouns via verbal nouns* to *participles*. They do not find it systematic to distinguish the category lying on this line somewhere between *verbal nouns* and *participles* as *gerund*, but they suggest classing terminologically all the *-ing* items (other than *deverbal* and *verbal nouns*) as *participles* with different degrees of verbality.

They also point out to the discrepancy between the Latin and English grammatical schemes. According to them, what is in English traditionally described as *gerund* is a more complex phenomenon than the forms denoted by this term in Latin, as it covers both nonmodal and modal meanings which in Latin correspond to the forms of *gerund* and *gerundive* respectively:

(39) *There was no shouting, merry-making, waving of flags.* (CGEL, 1985:1292) – nonmodal, corresponding to the Latin *gerund;*

(40) *There was no mistaking that scream.* (CGEL, 1985:1292) – modal, corresponding to the Latin *gerundive.*

On the other hand, Latin *gerund* carries only nonmodal meaning (Latin *ars amandi* corresponds to the *the art of loving*), while items with modal meaning are termed *gerundive* (the verbal adjective which can be used predicatively like a noun: *amandum est* means *'we should/must love'*). 'This lack of correspondence between the English *gerund* and the traditional use of the term can be advanced as a further reason for rejecting the term *gerund* in English.' (CGEL, 1985:1292)

Furthermore, according to them, 'there is potential ambiguity not only along the modal/nonmodal dimension, but also along the (traditional) *gerund/deverbal-noun* dimension' (Quirk et al, 1985:1292), when one sentence can be interpreted in the following ways:

(41) *There is no writing on the blackboard today.* (CGEL, 1985:1292)

modal *gerund* – We can't write on the blackboard (because we have no chalk).
nonmodal *gerund* – We are not going to write on the blackboard (since all our work is going to be oral)
nonmodal *deverbal noun* – There is nothing written on the blackboard.
The authors thus avoid the binary distinction of *gerund* and *participle* as being non-systematic.

The *-ing* forms ranking with Group 1 are referred to as *deverbal nouns* representing concrete count nouns derived from the verb. Group 3 *-ing* forms denoting abstract noncount nouns are termed *verbal nouns*. Group 4 and 5 *-ing* forms are terminologically classed as *participles* while the authors admit that instances in Group 4 showing a mixture of nominal and verbal characteristics in the *-ing* form have been traditionally referred to as *gerunds*, while Group 6 are *verbs*.

In respect of the terminology relating to the structural status of *-ing* forms, the authors refer to Groups 1, 2 and 3 as constituents of noun phrases while Group 4 and 5 representatives are constituents of nonfinite clauses. There is some confusion as to Group 4 *-ing* forms which are not complemented or modified when they are structurally interpreted as heads of noun phrases. Group 6 *-ing* forms are referred to as 'the purely participial form' which are constituents of 'finite verb phrases' (CGEL, 1985:1290).

In his study on the occurrence of non-finite forms clauses in the Chaucers' works (to-infinitival, *-ing* participial and *-ed* participial) Quirk excludes what we term gerundial and verbal-noun *-ing* forms form his considerations although admitting that "In Chaucerian English as in modern, there is no obvious and (still less) no linguistically orthodox point at which the convenient unit 'clause' ceases and another convenient unit (say, 'phrase') begins. The decision on segmentation is taxonomically arbitrary one and depends on the selected criteria and the purpose of the analysis." (Quirk, 1995:95)

Colen, A., (1984)
The author attempts to oppose the general definition of *nominalisations* stipulated by the generative grammar, namely the fact that in order to qualify as a *nominalisation* a construction must satisfy two conditions simultaneously: it must function as a nominal constituent within the sentence, and it must have an internal structure and/or syntactic characteristics which are not typical of nouns and noun phrases *ie* they have the internal syntactic structure of sentences. According to her, "*nominalizations* function not as noun phrases, but as complements to verbs (and to predicative elements in general), and that they have internal structure not of sentences but of predicative phrases." (Colen, 1984:36) Like a noun phrase, a *nominalisation* does not constitute a message

(which is the basic function of the sentence, *ie* a sentence represents the grammaticalisation of a minimal unit of information). The *nominalisation* "becomes communicatively meaningful only when it functions as an element within a sentence. ... it is, by definition, embedded in larger constructions in which it fulfils a specific nominal function." (Colen, 1984:20) She therefore concludes that *nominalisations* are "*predicative phrases* which are embedded in sentences... as obligatory dependents of the predicator. The term '*predicative complement to the predicator*' is more accurate than the term '*nominalization*'." (Colen, 1984:36)

Greenbaum, S., (1973)
Greenbaum adopts Chomsky's terminology and distinguishes between *gerundive nominals* which are derived by "a grammatical transformation from an underlying sentence-like structure"(Chomsky,1970:187), and the *adverbial -ing participle clauses* which may or may not be introduced by a conjunction, *eg:*

(42) *Since refusing the offer, John hasn't been to see us.* (Greenbaum, 1973:1)

(43) *Having removed his jacket and tie, he lay down on the bed.* (Greenbaum, 1973:8)

In this treatise the author concentrates mainly on the latter type, and he analyses the factors influencing the possibility of nonfinitisation of a finite subordinate clause into a nonfinite *-ing* participle clause (syntactically functioning as adverbial).
He reserves the term *derived nominals* for the nouns derived from verbs, *eg:*

(44) *Before their stay in New York, they often visited their parents.* (Greenbaum, 1973:3)

Mair, Ch., (1988)
In his paper the author presents results of his research into extraposed gerundial subject clauses in present-day British English. He investigated the Corpus of the Survey of English Usage (University College London) to survey the occurrence of extraposed gerundial subject clauses and compare it with that of the analogical type of infinitival clauses. Mair treats gerunds separately from participles and assigns the constructions which are headed by them a clausal status. His research shows that while "extraposition is the statistical norm for infinitival subject clauses... with gerundial subject clauses, on the other hand, extraposition is not as common and subject to many constraints." (Mair, 1988:52) The author analyses this issue from several perspectives: the stylistic –

extraposed gerundial subject clauses are more frequent in spoken and informal language; lexico-morphological – the presence of a verbal (rather than a nominal or adjectival) matrix predicate tends to prevent gerundial extraposition, it is more frequent after certain matrix predicates such as *be + no good/no use/worth/fun*; prosodic – the matrix predicate and the extraposed gerundial subject "appear as two separate tone units with a very short pause or no pause in between." (Mair, 1988:57); and syntactic – the potential overlap between extraposition, right dislocation and adverbial interpretation of the sequence under review:

(45) *It's all right living in such a house with a husband who's handy.* (Mair, 1988:58)

… (possible interpretation – *if you live…*),

due to which the author finds this type of structure indeterminate between the above three syntactic interpretations, combing traits of all of them.

Gove, P., (1965)
The author finds the gerund-participle dichotomy unnatural to English. In his article he attempts to advice lexicographers when an *-ing* forms should be given a separate entry in a dictionary, *ie* when it is necessary to treat it as a full noun or adjective: "grammatical analysis can easily ignore the boundary lines between gerunds and nouns and between participles and adjectives. It is sufficient to specify which a given form in a given context is. But a dictionary maker must generalize and synthetize and make a positive decision on whether to enter a word if a noun or adjective or omit if a gerund or participle." (Gove, 1965:40) It is suggested that no special entry should be reserved for an *-ing* form if its meaning is equivalent to any of senses listed in the infinitival entry for the verb or if it is corresponding to action nouns formed by suffixes other than *-ing*. The author tries to separate semantic sub-classes of *-ing* forms within the word-class of nouns and adjectives which, however, contradicts his initial maxim as the meaning, (and also the syntactic status itself), of an *-ing* form is always contextually dependent.

Wonder, J. P., (1970)
The author applies the term *gerund* to both the variants of Group 3 and 4 *-ing* forms.

Table 2. Terminology employed by the authors cited in this study.

	Group 1 and 2	Group 3	Group 4	Group 5	Group 6
Quirk	deverbal noun	verbal noun	Participle	participle	participle
Trnka	*-ing* forms	*-ing* forms	*-ing* forms	*-ing* forms	*-ing* forms
Jespersen, Curme	-------	nominal gerund	verbal gerund	participle	participle
Mathesius, Hais, Vachek, Hladký, Firbas, Dušková	deverbal noun	verbal noun	gerund	participle	participle
Marková		verbal noun	true verbal gerund		
Lees	3rd nominal concrete noun	1st nominal action nominal	2nd nominal gerundive nominal		
Kjellmer,Wonder		gerund	gerund		
Chomsky, Greenbaum		mixed form	gerundive nominal		

We assume that it is the specific combination of the morphological and syntactic potential of the respective groups of *-ing* forms which accounts for a somewhat unique character of each of them. In order to indicate specific morphological and syntactic properties of which an *-ing* form is capable we shall employ the following terminology commonly used in the Czech and Slovak English linguistics:

Group 1 – *deverbal nouns;*
Group 2 – *non-ing-verbal nouns;*
Group 3 – *verbal nouns;*
Group 4 – *gerunds;*
Group 5 – *participles;*
Group 6 – *nonfinite verb forms.*

2.3 Characteristics of the *-ing* groups as to morpholy and structure

The labelling as such, of course, does not solve the problem whether all of the respective types may be actually assigned a separate word class status. The types termed verbal nouns, gerunds and participles seem to be mixing up different degrees of nominal and verbal properties.

The morphological characteristics of deverbal nouns, non-*ing*-verbal nouns and -*ing* verbal nouns is almost identical except that -*ing* verbal nouns do not admit plural inflection. The forms function as heads of noun phrases and perform the syntactic functions typical of noun phrases.

The difference between the groups of deverbal nouns and verbal nouns consists in the fact that the former are pure nouns whose relation to the original verbal base loosened in terms of semantics as well as syntax: "they lack verbal features: they are not names of actions, they do not imply a subject and do not express predication" (Marková, 1986:89), all of these features are, however, related to verbal noun representatives. Verbal nouns, on the other hand, have inherent predicative character – "they comprise secondary predication" (Dušková, 1988:542), they have "underlying sentence-like structure" (Chomsky, 1970:187) and they operate as sentence condensers, regardless of the explicit presence of the subject and/or other elements of clause structure.

Basically we assume that where an -*ing* form is primarily used to denote rather than to predicate a certain activity, state or property to a subject then it may be ranked with deverbal nouns.

As has been suggested, withinn the category of verbal nouns there are distinguished two subgroups denoting two shades of meaning: action viewed as process *vs* concept/fact/single completed act. These two shades of meaning are usually conveyed by nouns derived from the original verbal base by means of two different suffixes. The former being rendered by
-*ing* verbal nouns while the latter by those derived by suffixes other than -*ing*, *eg: -al*, *-ature*, *-ion*, *-age etc* (Chomsky's derived nominals). Thus while the noun phrases *the passing of an Act, the committing of an offence* should convey the former meaning, the noun phrases *the passage of an Act, the commission of an offence* should serve as instances of the latter meaning, and we assume that they may not be used interchangeably:

(46) *Section 65 and this section come into force on the* ***passing*** *of this Act.* (FLA)

(47) *Slightly more than 5000 boats were registered with the Coast Guard prior to the recent* ***passage*** *of the state boating law.* (Brown Corpus)

With some verbs, however, the two derivational variants are not available and both meanings are expressed by the -*ing* form variant. A simple table exemplifies the point:

Table 3. Exemplification of *-ing* verbal nouns *vs* verbal nouns derived by other suffixes.

	borrow	make	dispose	Pass	commit
1.process	borrowing	making	disposing	passing	committing
2.action in general or a single act	borrowing	making	disposal	passage	commission

Verbal nouns carrying the latter meaning are morphologically, semantically, and in the following examples also in respect of their syntactic function, equivalent to nouns formed by suffixes other than *-ing* (*-al* and *-ment* in the examples below):

(48) *Marital proceedings come to an end-*
(a) *on the* ***making*** *of a separation order,*
(b) *on the* ***making*** *of a divorce order,*
(c) *on the* ***withdrawal*** *of the statement by a notice in accordance with section 5(3)(a), ...* (FLA)

We may therefore assume that when there do not exist two derivational variants of nouns derived from one verbal base, the *-ing* form variant may convey both meanings and it is the context that shall indicate either of them as in (49) and (50):

(49) *If after* ***the making of*** *a divorce order or* ***the grant of*** *a decree annulling a marriage either spouse remarries, that spouse is not entitled to apply, by reference to the making of that order or the grant of that decree, for a Part II order.* (FLA)

(50) *... and this subsection shall apply in relation to the* ***making****, acceptance, endorsement, alteration, cancellation or destruction in whole or in part of a valuable security, and in relation to the* ***signing*** *or* ***sealing*** *of any paper or other material in order that it may be made or converted into, or used or dealt with as, a valuable security, as if that were the execution of a valuable security.* (TA)

In our study we distinguish the non-*ing* verbal nouns and *-ing* verbal nouns.

Gerunds and participles show the mixture of nominal and verbal properties due to which they cannot be clearly ranked either with nouns or verbs. As it is clear from the table they cannot have plural ending, articles, demonstrative pronouns, adjective premodification, and *of*-construction postmodification.

The ability to function as prepositional complement seems to be one of the factors that distinguish the gerundial *-ing* forms from the participial ones the representatives of which may be introduced by a conjunction.

The verbal potential shared by both groups may be characterised by the adverbial modification, preservation of verbal government, aspect (perfect/non-perfect) and voice contrast, *eg:*

(51) *Its having been drawn rapidly does not detract from its value.* (Dušková, 1988:570)

(52) *I suspect him of having made it up.* (Dušková, 1988:570)

The capability of participial *-ing* forms to potentially show the progressive/nonprogressive aspect contrast (which is neutralised when the *-ing* form functions as a modifier), seems to be another feature that accounts for a distinct character of the two of the groups, *eg:*

(53) *Having been reading till long after midnight, I felt rather sleepy in the morning.* (Dušková, 1988:270)

The subject of the action specified may have the form of the possessive case only with the gerundial *-ing* forms, but even in this case it alternates with common or objective case without any difference on the semantic level. The subjective case of pronouns for gerundial *-ing* forms is also possible when the gerundial *-ing* form is the subject, *eg:*

(54) *They being my friends makes the matter somewhat awkward.* (Dušková, 1988:572)

Few comments should be made in relation to the use of the possessive *vs objective/common case* with the gerunds. First we should like to discuss the possessive case. When we compare its semantics and the function in the construction of which it is a part we find considerable differences in the following examples:

(55) *His drawings fascinate me.* (Dušková, 1988:569)

(56) *His rapid drawing of the picture fascinated me.* (Dušková, 1988:569);

(57) *His drawing the picture so rapidly fascinated me.* (Dušková, 1988:570)

The possessive case occurs within a noun phrase (here headed by deverbal nouns and verbal nouns) and with gerunds. There is, however, a difference in the semantic interpretation of the possessive case in the three examples supplied here. From the semantic point of view, it expresses the proper possessiveness (*ie* "the possessives primarily denote the possessor of the object referred to by the head noun" (Dušková, 1999a: 260)) only in (55) when the *-ing* refers to the result of the action, while instances (56) and (57) referring to the action itself suggest an agentive interpretation of the possessive case. We may observe the impact of different semantic interpretation of the possessive case on its functional interpretation: in (55) it has a *prima facie* determinative function in the noun phrase (determinative function is understood here as the function of an element in a noun phrase which determines "what kind of reference a noun phrase has" (CGEL,1985:64)), in (56) it still performs a determinative function within a noun phrase although there may be observed a shift from the possessive to agentive meaning, whereas in (57) the said shift, underlined by the following gerund, is present so strongly that it invites a question whether its agentive meaning still allows of its syntactic function being interpreted as determination or whether it resembles more of the function of the subject of a verbal element which it shares identical semantic role with. The use of the possessive case to express the agent of the action conveyed by the *-ing* form represents one of the features which indicate the gradient syntactical status of the constructions headed by the gerundial *-ing* forms.

Turning to the objective case of pronouns/common case of nouns in the same position its semantic role is obviously to express the agent of an action conveyed by the *-ing* forms and it is used with gerunds as well as participles, *eg:*

(58) *Mother always insisted on us/(the family) having a party at Christmas.* (Dušková, 1988:573)

In such constructions the objective case of pronouns or the common case of nouns represents syntactically the object of the finite verb phrase and at the same time it is the subject of the *-ing* form. It is evident that the objective/common case does not perform the determinative syntactic function, but that of the subject of the verbal element.

The common case subject of the *-ing* form is said to have gained frequency around 1700, according to Jespersen, as "a natural native development" (Jespersen, 1965e:122) justified mainly by the fact that in some cases in was impossible or, at least, quite difficult to form the possessive case (group of words, inanimate subjects, demonstrative pronouns *etc*). The most resistant to this usage was the category of personal pronouns: first instances of *it* instead of *its* were found "in isolated examples as early as the beginning of the eighteenth century, but *its* has never ceased to be the form most frequently used." (Jespersen, 1965e:133) The oblique case of the rest of personal pronouns is first recorded another century later. Similarly, *there* as subject of an *-ing* is substantially recorded only in the 19th century.

As to the tension between the preference for the possessive *vs* common/objective case with the gerundial *-ing* forms Dušková (Dušková, 1988:572) points to the fact that the possessive case is traditionally considered as more appropriate here from the structural point of view. When for example the *-ing* form occurs in the construction which functions as the subject of a finite verb, in relation to this verb the *-ing* form acquires a status of the head determining its form, while it behaves as a dependent item in relation to a non-possessive case, *eg:*

(59) *Women saying things like that* revolts me. (Dušková, 1988:572); *versus*

(60) *Women's saying things like that* revolts me. (Dušková, 1988:572).

Even when the *-ing* form occurs in a position of an object of the finite verb the genitive is suggested as preferable, the objective case being deemed as *fused participle* (Dušková, 1988:573), *eg:*

(61) *You may depend on my/me not mentioning it.* (Dušková, 1988:573)

Trnka (1956:105) suggests a semantic factor that might play a role in the preference for the genitive *vs* objective case: the use of the genitive subject may sometimes lead to the strengthening of a nominal sense of the *-ing* form, *eg:*

(62) *He did not care about their learning.* (Trnka, 1956: 105)

while the variant with the objective case of the pronoun *they*, namely:

(63) *He did not care about them learning.* (Trnka, 1956: 105)

would seem more verbal from the semantic point of view.

He further paraphrases Curme that constructions with objective/common case are typical of colloquial speech and Northern dialect of English while the possessive is preferred in the literary language, which may indicate that there are stylistic reasons as well as those concerning the geographical variants of English which might play a role in the selection of either variant.

The following is a summary of factors accounting for a traditional preference in favour of the possessive and objective/common case respectively as found in the works of Dušková (Dušková,1988:572-574, 1999b:25-26), Quirk *et al.* (CGEL, 1985:1063), Biber *et al.* (Biber, 1999:749-751), Trnka (Trnka, 1956:105-106) and Jespersen (Jespersen, 1966:320-328).

The possessive case is preferred where:

- the subject is a personal pronoun
- the subject has a personal reference or is a proper noun
- the style is formal
- the gerundial construction appears in the subject position and its subject is a personal pronoun, *eg:*

(64) *My forgetting her name was embarrassing.* (CGEL, 1985:1064)

(65) *Harriet's staying away so long was beginning to make her uneasy.* (Trnka, 1956:106)

The instance (65), however, also allows of common case (Trnka, 1956:106). Jespersen treats the oblique case in this type as "half vulgar" (Jespersen, 1965e:136), *eg*:

(66) *What pleased them far more than anything was me knowing them by their Christian names.* (Jespersen, 1965e:138)

(67) *Him hanging around like this, just messing things up, don't fit in anywheres that I can see.* (Jespersen, 1965:139)

- the meaning should acquire more nominal character
- when the attention should be focused on the action described rather than on the agent, *ie*:

(68) *I appreciate your being here.* (Biber, 1999:750)

The objective/common case is preferred where:

- the subject is not a pronoun,
- the subject is a pronoun which does not have a possessive form: *this, that, all etc*
- the subject does not have a personal reference

(69) *His mother kicked a little at first against the money's having gone to him.** (Jespersen, 1966:325)

(70) *There is a chance of some record being left.* (Jespersen, 1966:324)

- one of the words joined in the construction is a personal pronoun, *eg*:

(71) *There was no need of both of them making a journey.* (Jespersen, 1966:325)

(72) *Some remark about my patient and me being well qualified to keep each other company.* (Jespersen, 1966:325)

- the subject is inanimate or abstract noun (*possibility, chance...*) and when the subject is indefinite (*a man, people, anybody*), *eg*:

(73) *I am unhappy at that consolation being withdrawn.* (Dušková, 1999b: 25)

(74) *He insists on no one knowing about the experiment.* (Jespersen, 1966:326)

- the style is not formal
- the subject is in plural, *eg*:

(75) *Mrs Bennet, who had calculated on her daughters remaining at Netherfield* – ... (Jespersen, 1966:324, citation from Jane Austin)

- the singular possessive form is avoided since it is homophonous with the plural, *eg*:

(76) *I don't approve of my son's doing that.* (Dušková, 1999b:25)

- the construction is lengthy and would normally require a group genitive or simply the word-group cannot be used in the possessive, *eg*:

(77) *Do you remember the students and teachers protesting against the new rule?* (CGEL, 1985:1064)

(78) *Upon my application for her address being refused, I had resigned my own post.* (Jespersen, 1966:324)

- the subject of the *-ing* form is postmodified, *eg:*

(79) We can't *risk the only remaining typist in the office falling ill.* (Dušková, 1988:574)

- to avoid two genitives following each other, *eg*:

(80) *There ought to be a law against a man's sister ever entering his house after he's married.* (Jespersen, 1965e:131)

- an adverb is placed between the subject and the *-ing*, *eg*:

(81) *She liked to think of Trafford very rapidly and easily coming forward into a position of cardinal significance.* (Jespersen, 1965e:131)

- the emphasis should be on the pronoun rather than on the *-ing*, *eg*:

(82) *Fancy me being as old as any two of you.* (Jespersen, 1965e:134)

(83) *Instead of me talking to you, you ought to be talking to me.* (Jespersen, 1965e:134)

In the last two examples the possessive pronoun would be weakly stressed.

Dušková states that "observations of usage have shown that possessive forms are more frequent with personal pronouns than with nouns…, whereas the non-possessive form prevails overwhelmingly with nouns." (Dušková, 1999b:26). Jespersen objects to to many theorists holding that the use of the objective case of a personal pronoun instead of the possessive is incorrect as "it still can be found in good writers" (Jespersen, 1966:326). As for the variants *its/it* in this position the former seems to be more frequent according to Jespersen.

The above notes apply to the case where the gerundial and participial structures comply with the criterion to express overtly the subject of the *-ing* form which is not identical in reference with the subject of the finite verb in the main clause – so called *attachment rule* (CGEL, 1985: 1121). The agent of the *-ing* form, however, does not necessarily have to be expressed: "No indication is needed in the numerous cases in which the subject is either the 'generic person' or identical with something mentioned in the main sentence, …" (Jespersen, 1966:323). The omission of an explicit agent of the action denoted by the *-ing* form may be interpreted in two ways:

1. its explicit expression would be semantically redundant for one of the following reasons:
    a) it is identical in reference with the agent of the finite verb in the active voice, *eg:*

(84) *He denies knowing anything about it.* (Dušková, 1988:573)

or in the passive voice, *eg*:

(85) *The day was spent in packing.* (Jespersen, 1965e:141)

b) it is identical in reference with the object of the finite verb, *eg:*

(86) *Not having enough money taught her to economize.* (Dušková, 1988:571)

c) it is implied by the context or extralinguistic situation, *eg*:

(87) (My/ your/ our *etc.*) *Putting it off won't make things easier.* (Dušková, 1988:571)

2. its omission implies a general agent, *eg:*

(88) *Seeing is believing.* (Dušková, 1988:572)

Jespersen notices that "what purists may consider an inexact construction the understood subject is not the grammatical subject of the sentence but the natural agent of the action concerned." (Jespersen, 1965e:141)

Where none of the above applies and the attachment rule is violated, the structure is often criticised as a *dangling participle,* (other terms to denote it are *unattached, wrongly attached, pendant, suspended or unrelated participle* (Dušková, 1988:585). The whole construction is according to CGEL (1985:1222) more admissible (or less objectionable) if:

1. the subject is expressed in the matrix clause in some way, *eg:*

(89) *Having established a basis of this theory, the*/our next step is to analyse the structure and properties of the components.* (Dušková, 1988:586)

2. the *-ing* form is a component of a construction functioning as a style disjunct that comments on the style or form of what is said in the matrix clause, *eg:*

(90) *Putting it mildly, you have caused us some inconvenience.* (CGEL, 1985:1122)

(91) *Broadly speaking, the direct method is based on the situational approach.* (Dušková, 1988:584)

3. the implied subject is the whole of the matrix clause, *eg:*

(92) *The siren sounded, indicating that the air raid was over.* (CGEL, 1985:1122).

4. the implied subject is to be identified with *I, we,* and *you* of writer(s) or reader(s) in formal scientific writing (it has been institutionalised), *eg:*

(93) *When treating patients with language retardation and deviation of language development, the therapy consists, in part, of discussions of the patient's problems with parents and teachers, with subsequent language teaching carried out by them.* (CGEL, 1985:1123)

Dušková supplies two variants of this constructions: the subject of the sentence is *it* or *there, eg*:

(94) *Referring to reaction it will be seen that three distinguishing features of dissociative recombination are:...* (Dušková, 1999b:21)

or the subjects of the finite verb and the participle are different, but that of the participle is not expressed, *eg*:

(95) *Something, possibly, could be done – measures should, perhaps be taken – whilst awaiting the arrival of the doctor.* (Dušková, 1999b:21).

According to Dušková, "the common feature (*of the dangling participle*) is that it can be transformed into an adverbial clause with an indefinite or general subject or with the passive voice." (Dušková, 1999b:21) Considering that unexpressed reference of the construction is general or indefinite as well as that fact that dangling participles function as adverbials which "generally display looser syntactic dependence than *eg* object" (Dušková, 1999b:22), Dušková does not regard this structure as objectionable, demonstrating also that it is not restricted only to scientific writing.

Dušková further finds that "Like the participle, the gerund may have an indefinite or general subject which is likewise not expressed." (Dušková, 1999b:22) She refers to this construction as "dangling, unattached, suspended gerund" (Dušková, 1999b:23), and she again underlines that the structure is unobjectionable and that "The capacity of these forms to imply an indefinite or general subject without actually expressing it may be one of the causes of their expediency... as a flexible device of complex condensation of the English sentence...". (Dušková, 1999b:23)

Similarly Curme: "This construction is usually censured by grammarians, but on account of its easy formation it is in wide use and is even approved natural English expression wherever the reference is quite general and indefinite: 'Generally *speaking* (= If *one* may speak in a general sense), boys are a nuisance.'" (Curme, 1980a:211) Curme ranks this construction with "absolute participles" (Curme, 1980b:158): one type of which is represented by those constructions where the subject is identical with that of the principal proposition, the other type is conceived as having an indefinite subject. Curme also points to the fact that this type of construction became a source for the prepositional syntactic re-interpretation of certain *-ing* forms, such as *regarding, including*.

Another structural variant with regard to the subject of the action conveyed by an *-ing* form is the type referred to as *absolute structure, absolute clauses* (CGEL, 1985:1120), *absolute participial structures* (Dušková, 1988:585) or *absolute nominative* (Curme, 1980:152b). Here the action in the *-ing* form has an overt subject expressed by a common case of a noun or a subjective case of a pronoun in the situation where it is not identical in reference with the subject of the finite verb in the superordinate clause. Such constructions "are not explicitly bound to the matrix clause syntactically." (CGEL, 1985:1120) Curme holds that "an absolute nominative, i.e., a nominative without grammatical relations to the principal proposition, is often used in English, ... in adverbial clauses and subject clauses." (Curme, 1980b:152-160)

(96) *Women having the vote reduces men's political power.* (Curme, 1980b:157)

(97) *He saying he is sorry alters the case.* (Curme, 1980b:157)

(98) *She and her sisters both being sick makes hard work for the rest of the family.* (Curme, 1980b:157)

(99) *No further discussion arising, the meeting was brought to a close.* (CGEL, 1985:1120)

(100) *He led the way down the road, his shadow stretching behind him on the grass.* (Dušková, 1988:585)

Jespersen treats this phenomenon under the heading 'nexus terciary' suggesting that it was introduced "at an early period in imitation of the Latin construction." (Jespersen, 1965e:45). Its frequency increased in the second Middle English period: it occurs in Chaucer, especially in his translations from Latin. Quirk's study on the occurrence of participial clauses in Chaucer demonstrated this tendency: "Finally, we can note 'source conditioning' such as the strikingly high proportion of participial verb clauses (in participial absolute constructions) in Boece, undoubtedly influenced by the corresponding constructions in the Latin model." (Quirk, 1995:111) The construction finally gained ground in the second half of the 17th century.

A prepositional variant of the *absolute structure* is introduced by the prepositions *with/without* the existence of which again somehow interferes with our attempt to clear-cut the dividing lines between the gerundial and participial constructions, *eg:*

(101) *Without anyone noticing, I slipped out of the room.* (CGEL, 1985:1124)

(102) *She's a bit lonesome poor thing, with her husband being so much away.* (Trnka, 1956:110)

The structural status of the constructions comprising gerundial and participial *-ing* forms is on the gradient between phrases and clauses. We use the term *semi-clause constructions* to indicate our position which inclines to the interpretation of the structural status of the constructions of which these types of *-ing* forms are a part as being the matter of syntactic gradience between the phrase and clause rather than that of syntactic ambiguity between the phrase and the clause.

Despite the semantic similarity (if not identity) of the possessive *vs.* objective/common case *ie* denotation of the agent of the action – they attribute a different structural quality to the *-ing* form following it and thus their respective use carries along different structural interpretations of the structures they are a part of. While the presence of the possessive ranks the structure comprising the *-ing* form with noun phrases, the occurrence of the common/objective case assigns the construction a transient structural status placing it somewhere between a phrase and a clause. Lack of uniformity as for the definite linguistic rules governing the occurrence of either of them indicates the fact that this is the area where the transition processes (from nouns to verbs) become manifested.

According to Quirk *et al.*: "We may classify a unit either on the basis of its form *eg* its internal structure, as a noun phrase, or as a verb phrase, or on the basis of its function *eg* as a subject or an object of a clause. A formal classification takes account of how a unit is composed of smaller units or components."(CGEL, 1985:48-49) The formal categories which we are going to examine in this respect are *phrases* and *clauses* which represent units of two subsequent layers of the structural hierarchy of the sentence. The *phrase,* according to Quirk *et al.,* "is named after a class of word which has a primary, and indeed obligatory function in it." (CGEL, 1985:60). The authors recognise five formal categories of phrases: verb phrases, noun phrases, adjective phrases, adverb phrases and prepositional phrases. The criterion of difference between the phrase and the clause for Quirk *et al.* (here we are concerned with the structure comprising a gerund or participle) is the capability *vs* incapability of the structure to be analysed into clause elements. We observed this criterion in their analysis of 'nominal *-ing* clauses'. (CGEL, 1985:1064-65) They further suggest a semantic factor, namely the mode and nonmode interpretation of the construction, where the former should be an indicator of the phrasal status while the latter should be an indicator of the clausal status of the structure.

According to Quirk *et al.*,(1985) the two suggested criteria for the phrasal status are as follows:

1. incapability of the construction of being analysed into elements of a clause structure
2. mode interpretation (CGEL, 1985:1065), which is exemplified in (85):

(103) *They liked* ***our singing***. (CGEL, 1985:1065),

whereas the presence of the opposite features *ie* the capability of the construction of being analysed into clause elements and nonmode interpretation would attribute clausal status to the construction, *eg*:

(104) *They liked* ***us singing*** *(while they worked).* (CGEL. 1985:1065)

(105) *They liked* ***our singing folk songs***. (CGEL, 1985:1065)

Hence, (103) is, according to the authors, structurally a noun phrase while structures exemplified in (104) and (105) are nominal *-ing* participle clauses.

As was mentioned above the representatives of gerundial and participial *-ing* forms show an obscure character with regard to the word class to be ranked with due to the fact that the mixture of their verbal properties (modification by an adverb, subject of the action detached absolutely, preservation of verbal government, occurrence after a conjunction *etc*) and nominal properties (possessive case as determiner, syntactic role of subject/object, occurrence after a preposition *etc*) is so specific that the resulting construction is anomalous if compared with any of the well-established word classes. Therefore ranking these types of *-ing* forms with neither the word class of nouns nor verbs seems adequate and consequently the construction of which they are obligatory constituents can be named after neither of these formal classes. Quirk *et al.* (1985) dwell on the 'syntactic ambiguity' of this structure resulting in its dual interpretation of either its being a noun phrase, if the adverb and object is omitted and possessive determiner is present, or a nominal *-ing* participle clause especially with the subject in common case or objective case or when an object or adverbial is present, as the criterion of difference between the former and the latter for the authors is, as has been already mentioned, the capability/incapability of the structure to be analysed into clause elements and mode/nonmode semantic interpretation.

We assume that the first criterion is not fully applicable due to the fact that the possessive case here operates grammatically as a determiner, but its semantics suggests the reference to the agent of the action specified *ie* it is semantically the subject of the action specified. Even when there is no determiner the agent of the action is implicitly present as it may be inferred or comprised in external or sentential context, *eg:*

(106) *Her first job was selling computers.* (CGEL, 1985:1063).

Moreover, in most cases there is no semantic difference between the agent expressed in the possessive or common/objective case, the occurrence of either variant being subject to other than semantic criteria. Dušková admits that "Some authors seem to discern a difference in meaning or emphasis between *I am surprised at* ***his/him*** *saying so,* while others observe none." (Dušková, 1999b:26)

Similarly, neither the second criterion *ie* mode *vs* nonmode interpretation is of general validity. Wonder maintains that "the prescriptive use of the possessive case with the *-ing* form reinforces semantic ambiguity of the construction as it strengthens its manner (mode) reading, *eg*:

(107) *I understand Igor dancing.* (Wonder, 1970:263)

a) nonmode meaning: I understand it that Igor dances.

(108) *I understand Igor's dancing.* (Wonder, 1970:261)

a) nonmode meaning: I understand it that Igor dances.
b) mode meaning: Igor's dancing is understandable to me." (Wonder, 1970:263)

Where (107) is clearly factitive and (108) is ambiguous due to fact that "the genitive is structurally preferable but semantically equivocal. In popular usage the omission of *'s* clearly disambiguates the meaning of the *-ing* form in favour of the factitiveness." (Wonder, 1970:263) Thus the semantic criterion as an indicator of the phrasal or clausal status appears as unsatisfactory for the gerundial *-ing* forms are capable of expressing both mode as well as nonmode meanings notwithstanding the presence or omission of other elements of the clause structure in the construction of which they are a part, manner /factitive meaning of the structure depending upon the semantics of other constituents.

The above reasons should serve as the grounds for the assertion that all of the constructions comprising gerundial *-ing* forms have an underlying clausal character regardless of the form of their subject.

There is another discrepancy in the Quirk's *et al.* classification of *-ing* constructions. According to the authors, one distinguishing criterion between the word class of prepositions and conjunctions is that the former "introduce complements which are nominal or nominalized and the latter introduce subordinate clauses" (CGEL, 1985:660). On the other hand they admit that prepositions are capable of introducing nonfinite *-ing* clauses *eg:*

(109) *On arriving she took a taxi.* (CGEL, 1985:660)

(110) *I'm looking forward to meeting you.* (CGEL, 1985:659)

For us this is another factor to support the standpoint that the constructions comprising *-ing* forms cannot be clearly classified as clauses, but they are on the gradient between phrases and clauses.

As for the participial *-ing* forms they are usually treated as nonfinite forms of the word class of verbs. If we apply the criteria set in the previous paragraphs we find out that they lack any mode meaning and that the construction of which they are a part is capable of clausal analysis. Thus it seems that the clausal status of the constructions of which these *-ing* forms are constituents manifests itself clearly on this level and the criteria suggested by Quirk *et al.* (CGEL,1985:1065) seem to be applicable here.

The problem of the structural status of the gerundial and participial *-ing* forms has common grounds in their inherent clausal nature. We therefore hold that the status of such *-ing* forms is not the issue of *syntactical ambiguity* but that of *syntactical gradience between a phrase or a clause the latter being more clearly manifested in participial constructions.* (We, however, agree that constructions in the sentences like, *eg:*

(111) *They are busy preparing barbecue.* (CGEl, 1985:1063)

are ambiguous regarding the interpretation of the *-ing* forms as amounting to the gerundial or participial group, both interpretations remaining open as for their structural status).

Justification of the gradient structural status which we assign to the constructions headed by the gerundial or participial *-ing* forms invites some comments on the nominal trends in the English sentence.

We should start by the term *nominalisation* (the definition of which has already been provided in the introductory passage of the present work) used by Quirk *et al.* (to refer to "the noun phrases (or we had better use the expression to refer to the 'phenomenon' – to leave aside the issue of the structural definition of the constructions in question) the constituents of which have corresponding counterparts in the elements of semantically related clauses" (CGEL,1985:1288-89), *eg:*

(112) *The quarrel /their quarrelling over pay, (= They quarrelled over pay.) was the reason for his resignation.* (CGEL,1985:1288)

Basically the same position is maintained by the theory introduced by V. Mathesius. Mathesius asserts that although "the subject – verb predication is one of the most conspicuous features of the Indo-European languages, the nominal tendency is more or less ascertainable in all languages" (Mathesius, 1913:325-326). He refers to it as the nominal tendency in the verbal predication where the verbo-nominal form conveys the action which in another historical stage of the same language, or in another stylistic layer of the same language or in other languages is usually rendered by a pure verb. If English is to be compared in this respect with other Indo-European languages, Mathesius maintains that nominal trends are ascertainable also outside the scope of the literary style and the trend appears to be highly productive also in ordinary, colloquial language.

Mathesius further distinguishes between two variants in the English nominal trends: the *subjectless verbo-nominal predication* and the *subject verbo-nominal predication.* The former includes cases where the action is expressed by a nominal element accompanied by a verb conveying verbal grammatical categories and the genitive *of*-construction to express the subject (Dušková adds that it also may be the object if the form is derived from transitive verbs (Dušková, 1988:570)).

From the semantic point of view such constructions often express phenomenon which affects our senses and it is immaterial to analyse it into the action and the agent. It may be exemplified by the structures *there + be + nominal element (-ing form) + of-construction/a common case or objective case of pronouns, eg:*

(113) *There was a slamming of doors, a ringing of bells, and the voice of Mr. Heelas bellowing like a bull.* (Mathesius, 1913:328)

(114) *And there was no shouting after Kemp's cry – only a sound of blows and feet and a heavy breathing.* (Mathesius, 1913:328)

(115) *There shall be no burning, though that were deserved.* (Mathesius, 1913:329)

The latter variant – the *subject verbo-nominal predication* – is characterised by the presence of the subject and the verbal predicate which, however, is not expressed by a full verb, but by a copula and a noun, and it may be divided into *possessive class, eg : to have + a noun (to have a smoke), adverbial class, eg : to be/stand/fall/get/ + preposition + noun (to be in love, to be in a hurry),* and *causative class, eg: to do/ make/ give/ take /catch /fetch + noun (to do the cooking, to make a mistake, to give a shriek, to take leave, to catch a glimpse).*

Mathesius emphasised importance of the role played by the phenomenon of *complex condensation* which may be defined as "an introduction into a sentence of a nominal element or phrase (condenser) enabling the said sentence to do without a hypotactically or paratactically arranged clause the use of which would otherwise be indispensable." (Hladký, 1961:114). In this conception complex condensation is realised by special *means of complex condensation* (for short – condensers) some of which have already been suggested above. Condensers are mainly nominal forms derived from finite verbs, such as infinitives and various kinds of *-ing* forms (they distinguish between participles, gerunds and verbal nouns). Hence, even though the structures with the *-ing* forms have equivalents in clauses they are not considered as formations with an ellipsis of a finite verb, but that they assume the full syntactical status in the language system, and therefore represent constructions transient between the phrase and the clause, which cannot be clearly ranked either with phrases, or clauses. Their principal syntactical feature is the predicativeness. The *-ing* forms may or may not have an overt subject which can be expressed by the common case or subjective/objective case of pronouns or it may have the form of the possessive case, as has already been mentioned.

Condensers may also be approached from the point of view of the *functional sentence perspective.* The relatively high number of nominal elements in the English sentence results in the weakening of the dynamic character of the English finite verb, which confines itself only to expressing grammatical categories, while *communicative dynamism* is acquired by nominal elements. The term *communicative dynamism,* introduced by a Brno Anglicist J.Firbas, ranks with the terminology of *functional sentence analysis* arising from the functional definition of the sentence as an elementary reaction performed by means of language to any extra-lingual reality. While reacting to extra-lingual reality, the process of adding new pieces of information to the preceding store of information is taking place. This is manifested in the sentence as a rather clear distinction between its two parts: the *theme* or the basis of the sentence – the part or element about which the affirmation is effected, and the *rheme* or the nucleus of the sentence – the element effecting the affirmation. "The extent to which the sentence element contributes to the development of the communication is called '*communicative dynamism*'". (Firbas, 1961:97)

The existence of condensers reduces the *communicative dynamism* of the English finite verb (which in this context means the ability of the finite verb form to express predicated action or process in its totality: setting time, verbal aspect, mood along with the semantic) in that the semantic centre of gravity is shifted form the full verbal form on the nominal element whereas the function of the verb form is reduced to something that resembles a copula. This should also account for the fact that the English sentence is capable of expressing secondary predication by "dispensing with the finite verb form altogether, however vague its meaning might be" (Vachek, 1961:35).

Hladký maintains that if "the sentences containing condensers were 'discondensed' it would be necessary to introduce into them some formal words (conjunctions *etc),* and/or words conveying grammatical categories, already conveyed, however, by the subject and the finite verb" (Hladký, 1961:114), which regarding their FSP status are dynamically weak (representing a theme or transition). "Therefore an introduction of a condenser into a sentence also prevents repetition of some dynamically weak sentence elements." (Hladký, 1961:114).

According to Vachek, "if the sentence dispenses with a subordinate clause, this undoubtedly results in closer cohesion of its elements; such cohesion is equivalent to a greater condensity of the whole sentence structure." (Vachek, 1961:32).

Nonfinite forms of course constitute communicative subfields with their own FSP. Within a complex sentence, in the level of FSP they in fact operate in the same way as the subordinate clause(s) which within the FSP structure of the entire sentence belong either to the thematic or the rhematic section.

Summarising, we assume that the structural status of the constructions containing gerundial and participial *-ing* forms is on the gradient between phrases and clauses and therefore we shall be referring to them while interpreting their structural status as *semi-clause constructions,* availing ourselves of the term introduced by Mathesius in his treatise Řeč a sloh (Mathesius, 1966:72) while dealing with the apposition and transgressive. This term will be used to cover all of the constructions comprising gerundial and participial *-ing* forms notwithstanding the explicit capability or incapability of the whole structure of being analysed into clausal elements or the applicability of semantic criteria.

The *-ing* form regarded as verb (Group 6) in respect of morphology, semantics and predicative syntactic function is from the structural point of view the main verb of a complex finite verb phrase indicating the progressive aspect.

According to Quirk *et al.*, "Verb phrases consist of a main verb which stands alone as the entire verb phrase, or is preceded by up to four verbs in an auxiliary function." (CGEL, 1985:62) A simple chart taken from Quirk *et al.* (CGEL, 1985:62, 96, 149-154) shall demonstrate the possible functions of *-ing* forms in complex finite verb phrases:

Table 4. The *-ing* forms in the function of main verb.

	finite forms	*sank.*	
The ship		*was sinking.*	non-finite forms
		has been sinking.	
	must have been sinking.		(CGEL, 1985:62)
	auxiliaries	main verb	

Moreover, this type of *-ing* form may function as auxiliary indicating the progressive aspect of the passive, *eg:*

(116) *He might have been **being***$^{\textit{Auxiliary}}$ *questioned by the police.* (CGEL, 1985:121)

It may further indicate the progressive aspect of infinitive constructions that are traditionally ranked with semi-clause constructions, *eg:*

(117) *I'm glad to have been **working***$^{\textit{Head of infinitive semi-clause construction}}$. (CGEL, 1985:154)

3. *-Ing* forms in the projection of time (a diachronic approach)

The quest for the solution in respect of the word-class assignment of the forms under analysis is inevitably connected with tracing the processes that resulted in the currently available inventory of these forms and that could account for their present-day transitional status in terms of the above notes. The process of origination of these forms must be, in our opinion, distinguished from the way they are created nowadays. This is an obvious distinction between the diachronic and synchronic approaches to a certain linguistic phenomenon.

In the diachronic line we may speak of the word-formation processes as consisting of two stages: first, it was the word-formation mode known as derivation (whereby a suffix is added to a base), and second, the process referred to as functional shift (Jespersen's zero-derivation, Bauer's conversion, Štekauer's conceptual recategorisation). We find the diachronic approach rather instructive and explanatory (*eg* in respect of the combination of features that seem inadmissible today) serving to point to a basically common origin of all of these forms as well as to demonstrate their functional/syntactic specification which has taken place in the course of time and also its impact on the semantic and morphological character of the original form.

The diachronic tracing of the *-ing* form origination dates back to the existence of a verbal noun derived from a verbal base by the suffixes *-ung*, preferred in West Saxon, and the northern *-ing* in Old English of which the former "disappeared by about 1250" (Marchand, 1960:241) and the latter "eventually established itself as the Middle English norm, and so extended its range as to become one of the most important formatives, lexically and grammatically, throughout the history of late Middle English and New English." (Strang, 1970:338)

Jespersen suggests that "The history of the forms in *ing* is certainly one of the most interesting examples of the growth from a very small beginning of something very important in the economy of language." (Jespersen, 1972:182). Actually, as suggested by Jespersen, this suffix was originally added not to verbal bases but rather to nominal bases. The weak verbs were taken to be derivative bases for this process only by analogy that existed between some nouns and corresponding weak verbs. Adams points to the analogy between the Old English *weddung,* 'wedding,' the noun *wedd, 'pledge,'* and the verb *weddian.* "The Old English derivational suffix *-ing*, or *-ung*, was originally added, restrictedly, to nouns to form abstract nouns; but the nominal stems to which it was attached were subsequently taken to be those of weak verbs corresponding in form to them." (Adams, 1973:26) The repertory of verbal bases was extended to include strong verbs in late Old English (*breaking, fighting, drinking*) and also verbal bases borrowed from French in the 13th century (*serving, assailynge*). The growing deverbal capacity of these originally nominal suffixes enabled the coining of new substantives by means of a word-formation process, known as derivation, from weak verbs: "originally *-ung* from the second class (*hergung 'plunder'*), *-ing* from the first (*hering 'praising'*)." (Jespersen, 1965f:377) The same author holds that in early Middle English the former suffix prevailed extensively only to be replaced by the latter form in the subsequent period.

Examples of denominal bases to which the *-ing* ending was added may include the following: *scaffolding, shipping, clothing, westing* 'distance made towards the west', *easting* 'approach to an easterly direction'. The *-ing* suffix was added also to locative particles (*inning* 'income', *offing* 'off part, remote part'). In some cases it is not possible to determine whether the original base was verbal or nominal (*wadding*). (Marchand, 1960:242) Denominal suffixal nature of the *-ing* is demonstrated in Jespersen (1965f:101) by back-formation origination of some verbs from nominal formations *eg* currently popular verb *to caucus* was first recorded in 1850 whereas the recording of *caucusing* as a noun may be found already in 1788. In some cases a verb is formed from a corresponding substantive through a detour, *eg* the verb *to nut* ('gather nuts') was formed from the gerundial *go nutting* rather than from the noun *nut.* Another example may be the verb *to housekeep* whose base may have been *housekeep* or *housekeeping,* as pointed out by Jespersen (1972:165). In this respect Adams suggests that "nominal forms in *-ing* may be 'intermediaries' in the process of forming verbs, appearing at an earlier stage than the infinitive and the finite forms." (Adams, 1973:26) This may also be proved by non-existence of verbal counterparts of certain gerundial forms even in Modern English, *eg go mushrooming, blackberrying/to mushroom*, to blackberry*.*

The *-ing* form *ceiling* (first recorded in 1380), occurring in our corpus, is also an interesting example of back-formation *ie* the verb *ceil* was "obviously back-derived from it (*ceiling*) as it means furnish with a ceiling. A substantive *ceil** does not occur; obsolete *cyll* 'canopy', which is probably cognate with *ceiling*, is recorded 1552." (Marchand, 1960:242) Some authors might treat this *-ing* form as moneme.

The meaning of the resulting verbal nouns was denoting action as "the generic act, fact, practice of what the verbal idea implies." (Marchand, 1960:241) There were also formed derived nouns which conveyed "a specific instance of what the verbal idea implies, something material connected with the verbal idea *eg* agent, instrument, result, belongings, place." (Marchand, 1960:241) The suffix *-ung/-ing* thus accounts for the polysemy of these forms "from the earliest periods of the English language." (Marchand, 1960:241)

In this capacity the *-ing* ending may be ranked with other deverbal suffixes, *eg -ment, -a/ion, -al, -ure* which came from Latin through French. All of them were semantically associated with the verbal meaning: nouns ending in -*ure* denoted "action or process" and "later it came to mean also result of the action, and in some cases a collective body" (Jespersen, 1965f:244); *-ion* originally added in Latin to a passive participle denoted in English "action or process" (Jespersen, 1965f:372), *eg suggestion, selection; -ment* "was added to verbal stems, generally to denote the instrument, result, or product of an action, later also the action itself" (Jespersen, 1965f:375), *eg amendment, judgment;* the suffix *-al* added to Romanic end-stressed verbs "the act of *-ing* or state of being -ed" (Jespersen, 1965f:385), *eg acquittal, denial, refusal.*

According to Adams, it is quite natural to expect that the concrete meaning associated with *-ing* items is younger than the original 'action' meaning: "The following, denoting the action of the verb, are all dated by the Oxford English Dictionary in the fourteenth century: *drawing, failing, finding, meeting.* The related senses of 'picture,' 'defect,' 'discovery,' 'assembly' are recorded as occurring two or three hundred years later. The role of the *-ing* ending in these words in their later senses is just like that of noun-forming suffixes, such as *-ation* and *-ment*, and we may say that it is a derivational suffix here." (Adams, 1973:25) The former observation is also relevant to the discussion in section 4.

In the course of the 14th century the *-ing* derived verbal nouns started to occur in the constructions which combined nominal and verbal features *eg* Chaucer's *in suffringe paciently wronges* (cited in Vachek, 1994:224). "In its contrasts and in its functions the gerund has been growing steadily more verb-like, perhaps partly as a result of its formal identity and functional overlap with the *-ing* participle." (Strang, 1970:153)

The crucial distinction was the change of the form of object of the action conveyed by the *-ing* form. Prior to this change, there were only three possibilities: "the genitive case ('*sio feding para sceapa*', the feeding of the sheep), or it might form the first part of a compound (*blood-letting*), or, the usual construction in Middle English, it might be added after *of* (*in magnifying of his name*, Chaucer)... But from the fourteenth century we find a growing tendency to treat the ing like a form of the verb, and accordingly, to put the object in the accusative case. Chaucer's words, 'in getinge of your richesses and in usinge hem' show both constructions in juxtaposition." (Jespersen, 1972:184)

Another feature that gradually appeared in respect of this form was the possibility of its adverbial modification and also the capability to express the verbal distinction between perfect and non-perfect aspect and between the active and passive voice. While originally, similarly as the noun, this form was neutral as to time indication (and its simple form still is), since the end of the sixteenth century the form proceeded even further on its way to the verb, *ie* it developed a composite perfect. Shakespeare already distinguished its simple and perfect forms (*knowing* and *having known*) although not consistently so.

The passive gerund appears around 1600. Development of a new distinct passive gerundial form (employing the *being* auxiliary) was instigated by ambiguities arising from the inner potential of the form to render both active and passive meanings, *eg*:

(1) *Shall we... excuse his throwing into the water* (Jespersen, 1966:322, citation from Shakespeare)

(2) *Shall we excuse his being (or having been) thrown into the water?* (Jespersen, 1966:322)

The simple form can even today be construed passively in certain constructions, *eg*:

(3) *It wants mending.* (Jespersen, 1972:185)

Another quality which distinguished this form from the original *-ing* substantive was the form of the subject/agent. The pure noun denoting the action had subject in the possessive case. The new form retained this form of the subject especially in reference to an animate agent. Alongside there appeared instances where the subject was in the common case.

As Jespersen puts it: "Thanks to these extensions the *-ing* has clearly become a most valuable means of expressing tersely and neatly relations that must else have been indicated by clumsy dependent clauses." (Jespersen, 1972:186) With this new interpretation of the original verbal noun, the latter did not disappear, although its frequency tended to decrease in comparison with the gerund. It was reserved to express primarily the processuality of action.

Comparing the mode of origination of the *-ing* forms understood as verbal nouns and the new form respectively, we may conclude that while the former were formed by the process of derivation, the origin of the latter is based on a new interpretation of the morpho-syntactic potential of the original verbal noun accompanied by a semantic shift from substantival abstractness towards verbal concreteness and processuality. As the potential in question mixed up noun-like and verb-like characteristics the assignment of this form to either of the established word-classes seemed quite uncertain. Under the influence of Latin grammars a new term was employed to indicate its separate status, transitional between the noun and the verb, namely *gerund.* The functional shift accounting for the origination of the gerund *via* verbal noun was a gradual process running over centuries. The previous diachronic considerations may account for the persistence of mixed, and currently conceived as defective, constructions combining determination by articles/possessive case or adjective premodification of an *-ing* form with object complementation, *eg*:

(4) *Nothing in his life became him like* ***the leaving it****.* (Jespersen, 1966:323, citation from Shakespeare)

(5) *What else can joy be but* ***the spreading joy****?* (Jespersen, 1966:323, citation from Byron)

(6) *Provided that no Person who shall have claimed any Right to the Possession of such Child, or shall be the Mother or shall have claimed to be the Father of an illegitimate Child, shall be liable to be prosecuted by virtue hereof an account of* ***the getting Possession*** *of such Child, or taking such Child out of the Possession of any Person having the lawful charge thereof.* (Offences against the Person Act 1861, section 56).

(7) *On the way home (after returning the dog), he notices (for the first time) a poster announcing a CZK 5,000 reward for* ***the finding and returning the dog*** *he just returned.* (Chromá, 2003:371)

Another construction whose form is derived from the Old English verbal noun was so called *progressive form.* Originally, Old English started to express aspectual contrasts by means of a pair: simple finite verb form (which itself had a durative meaning) *versus* the verb *beon* + present participle, *eg se pe wip hine sprecende wæs,* (cited in Vachek, 1961:91). The latter construction was used to translate Latin *imperfectum* and it is "found sporadically in Old English (since the 9th century), but is at first something of an alien, a calque of Latin." (Strang, 1970:311) For Jespersen "... most of these expanded forms in translations render Latin verba deponentia: *locutus est = wæs sprecende, egressus est = wæs ferende...*" (Jespersen, 1965d:166). It was employed as an *ad hoc* construction to underline durativeness (mainly in the past) but its grammaticalisation did not occur in the period of Old English. Strang points only to the first genuine employments of this construction, independent of its Latin model, to convey the limited duration common with temporal expressions and also the recurrent/insistent action in that period.

The forms of the present participle varied: in the north it was formed by the ending *-ande,* in the Midlands by the ending *-ende* and in the south *-inde* (*lovande, lovende, lovinde*). "In later Middle English the ending *-ing* appears in the Midlands and the south, thus obscuring the dialectal distinction." (Baugh, 1957:229) The fusion of the *-i/ende* and *-ing* endings in the participial form in favour of the latter that started in the Midlands produced "a multiple-purpose form which is one of the most striking features of New English." (Strang, 1970:238)

The peripheral position of this periphrastic form is usually justified by the fact that the simple form of an Old English verb itself carried durative implications unless a prefix marked it as non-durative and it was only after decline of the old prefixal system when there arose a need of grammaticalisation of a new means to keep the aspectual contrast. To fill in the existing gap there was employed a construction of domestic origin, in contrast with the one based on analogy with Latin, namely the type making use of the verbal noun: *ic eom on huntunge* 'som na love,' (cited inVachek, 1961: 224), which was transferred to Middle English in a weak form as *I am a-hunting* and finally as *I am hunting.* This line of argumentation is present also in Jespersen (1965d) who justifies his position by the fact that there was a rather long time span between first records of the construction of the type *he wæs feohtende* in Old English and the more or less established usage of the construction *be + participle* to indicate aspectual distinction in the course of the 16th-17th centuries. Jespersen does not concur in opinion with Mossé who in his *Histoire de la forme périphrastique etre + participle present*, Paris, 1938 (cited in Jespersen, 1965e:415) supplies frequency data demonstrating the opposite, *ie* the statistic prevalence of the form *be + first participle* over the prepositional phrase *be + on + first participle,* defended by Jespersen, in Middle English period. Jespersen's main argument against Mossé seems to be inconsistent employment of the former as to the grammatical distinction the form was to indicate, namely 'frame-time implications' as opposed to non-durativeness. Curme states that "In Shakespeare's day the expanded form was used as today but not so often and so regularly: 'What *do you read* (now *are you reading*), my lord?' (*Hamlet,* II,ii)." (Curme, 1980:205)

In the beginning of the 16th century the *-ing* verbal noun form starts to be interpreted as *-ing* present participle ousting the former present participial form ending in *-ande/ende/inde* and completing the process of grammaticalisation of the verb *to be + present participle* to denote the progressive aspect of a verb. The period also brings about "... the development of a much fuller range of patterns, so that the periphrastic forms are almost fully symmetrical with the simple forms, and overall increase in frequency of usage far greater than the introduction of new patterns could account for." (Strang, 1970:207) Compound participles came into existence, according to Jespersen, in the 16th century, and the progressive passive (*the house is being build*) belong to the end of the 18th century.

The dropping of the preposition *on/in* in constructions with verbs other than *be* resulted in the syntactic functions currently treated as gerundial direct object (*begin a-creeping, keep a-puffing, fall a-laughing*), or adverbial of goal (*go a hunting*), participial adverbial object qualifier (*catch me on/in/a-/0 doing*). The construction *be busy (in) finding out* is currently capable of being identified as gerundial only by a diachronic reference to the former occurrence of the preposition that was dropped in the course of time, (examples in this paragraph taken from Jespersen, 1965d:169-174).

The functional use of the verbal participle was gradually extended to include the syntactic function of premodification and postmodification, and also that of the adverbial of various semantic roles (time, condition, concession, *etc*). In the last mentioned function it developed the nonperfect/perfect tense indication (the prefect form coming into existence in the 16th century) and then also the active/passive voice indication, recorded in the 17th century. On the other hand in the syntactic functions of premodification and postmodification aspectual indication of perfectivity was not established. When the *-ing* form penetrated to the premodifying syntactic function it started its way towards adjectivisation of some of its most frequent occurrences.

In respect of the adverbial syntactic function, one type of construction is directly accountable for by its Latin antecedent. Quirk's study on the Chaucer's use of non-finite clauses (1995) showed that *-ing* participial non-finite clauses prevailed in the adverbial syntactic function (Quirk, 1995:99) without but also with a separate subject:

(8) *And after this, nat fullich al awhaped,*
Out of the temple al esilich he wente,
Repentynge hym that he hadde evere ijaped
Of Loves folk (Chaucer, Troilus and Criseyde of the early 1380's cited in Quirk, 1995: 97)

(9) *And on the temple of dowves white and fayre*
Saw I syttynge many an hundred peyre (Chaucer, The Parliament of Fowls of the late 1370's or early 1380's cited in Quirk, 1995:102-103)

Tracing the occurrence of infinitival, *-ing* participial and *-ed* participial non-finite clauses in five extracts of Chaucer's works of approximately equivalent length, Quirk detected that one of them showed "a strikingly high proportion of participles, almost as many in fact as all the other texts taken together. ... These facts can probably be accounted for by reference to influence from Chaucer's Latin source." (Quirk, 1995:106). It was the text containing Chaucer's translation (of 1380) of Boethius' Latin *De Consolatione Philosophiae.*

This text also showed six out of all eight examples of adverbials with subjects in the common case as translations of the Latin ablative absolute constructions:

(10) *... the same Plato lyvynge, his mayster Socrates desserved victorie of unryghtful deth in my presence cf Latin eodem superstite* (Chaucer, Boece, 1380 in Quirk, 1995:109)

(11) *... and, the kyng knowynge of it, Y overcom it, so that the coempcioun ne was nat axid ne took effect cf Latin rege cognescente* (Chaucer, Boece, 1380 in Quirk, 1995:109)

These are usually termed *absolute participial constructions.* Regarding this form Jespersen (1965e) admits that it was quite rare in Old English occurring mainly in translations from Latin. Its frequency increased in the second part of Middle English (especially in the work of Chaucer), but not to the extent that it could be conceived as an already 'naturalised' construction. "But after 1660, when English prose style developed a new phase, which was saturated with classical elements, the construction rapidly gained ground and was finally naturalized in the language." (Jespersen, 1965e:46) In some of their most frequent realisations absolute participial constructions came to be treated as prepositions and conjunctions.

We may conclude this section by referring to its beginning *ie* from the historical perspective the current inventory of various types of *-ing* forms is diachronically linked with the Old English verbal noun derived first from nominal bases, then from verbal bases of weak verbs and subsequently those of strong verbs. Under various circumstances in the course of time there appeared a tendency to extend the syntactic scope of the original form. The new syntactic employment shaped the morpho-syntactic and semantic framework of the original form. The full naturalisation of a new employment of the *-ing* form with its new morho-syntactic and semantic potential could be attained only over a necessary period of time during which the frequency of the construction tended to increase.

4. Inflectional *versus* derivational nature of the *-ing* affix (a synchronic approach)

The synchronic point of view, derived principally from the recognition of these forms by their present users, suggests that there are currently existing several classes of these forms with a distinct semantic and morpho-syntactic potential. The question is, however, whether we can rank the process of their present-day creation within the framework of word-formation (the processes within this domain result in the formation of new lexemes) in all the types of *-ing* manifestations that we presented. We will attempt to settle this issue in the section dealing with the derivational *versus* inflectional character of the *-ing* ending.

Attempts to solve the issue of word-class assignment in respect of the possible representations of *-ing* forms have brought about a question whether the *-ing* affix is of derivative or inflectional nature. From the synchronic point of view the *-ing* affix (affix is treated here as a bound morph that can be added to a base to form new words or to a stem to form new word forms) shows a considerable functional overload. Its addition results in the formation of items that may be assigned the status of full nouns, verbs or adjectives, prepositions or conjunctions, and also the forms that we refer to as sentence condensers, *ie* verbal nouns, gerunds and participles. The process of formation of *-ing* forms is currently conceived as being effected by the addition of the *-ing* ending to a verbal base rather than in terms of the functional shift/conversion/zero derivation as described in the previous diachronic account. This rule, however, does not have universal applicability as the *-ing* affix cannot be added freely to any verbal base to form any of the above mentioned types of *-ing* forms without any restrictions. Another dimension relates to the fact that the resulting forms frequently show irregular character (also discussed as transitional or gradient) as to the testing that is usually employed to determine a particular word-class assignment (semantic, morphological and syntactic).

As suggested above, the status of an affix may be either inflectional or derivational. Derivation results in the formation of new lexical units while the process of inflection creates word forms. The function of derivation as one of the word-formation processes is to "generate new naming units designating extra-linguistic objects." (Štekauer, 1998:49) Inflection, on the other hand, "is considered to be a part of the Lexical Component, its function consists in providing a new naming unit, supplied from the Word-Formation Component, with morphosyntactic features depending on the respective paradigms to which they belong." (Štekauer, 1998:50). If the status of the *-ing* ending is suffixal the resulting *-ing* forms should be assigned a separate word-class status. If, on the contrary, the *-ing* is deemed an inflectional ending the output of its addition should result in the creation of a word-form, in this case a verbal word-form thanks to the verbal characteristics and underlying sentence-like structure of the constructions which are headed by these forms.

The question is how it is possible to distinguish the derivative nature of an affix from the inflectional. Being aware that the theoretical linguistic issue "inflection *versus* derivation" has been and, most probably, will be tackled by numerous authors concerned with the linguistic branches of morphology, lexicology and word-formation, and realising that a thorough account would exceed the scope of our present research, at this stage we should like to provide a limited and, inevitably, narrow exposition based on the summary of the criteria whose application may serve to distinguish inflection from derivation as we found it in Bauer (1983 and 2003). What Bauer basically does is contesting the various conditioning factors relevant to the issue in question as presented by his predecessors or contemporaries dealing with this problem. The author is contesting the following criteria:

- Inflection uses a closed set of affixes
- Inflectional morphology is what is relevant to syntax
- Derivational affixes are nearer the root than inflectional ones
- Derivatives can be replaced by monomorphemic forms
- Inflection is productive, derivation semi-productive
- Inflectional affixes have a regular meaning
- Derivation may cause a change of category

We attempted to subject the representatives of several types of *-ing*-forms to the above criteria. The following list of sentences comprising *-ing* items, and also forms created by the *-at/ure* ending included for the sake of comparison, may serve for the purposes of demonstration:

(1) *The Manager is authorised to bind the company with his sole **signature**.* (private instrument)

(2) *... total number of **signatures** not followed by ratifications:16; ...* (Chromá, 2003:443)

(3) *However, even if a particular contract requires a writing, this does not mean that both parties must sign it or that the **signing** occurs at the time of contracting.* (Chromá, 2003:377)

(4) *The United States, which has signalled its intention to ratify by formally **signing** the Convention, now stands as the only industrialized country in*

the world and one of only two United Nations member states yet to make this legal commitment to children. (Chromá, 2003:443)

(5) *Having signed the contract the party cannot revoke his/her offer without being subject to legal consequences.* (private instrument)

(6) *If there was an express agreement that the man who was* ***signing*** *was not to be liable, the section would not apply.* (Chartrand, 1997:92)

4.1 Inflection uses a closed set of affixes

Starting with the first criterion the closed system implies impossibility to add extra variables to a set of affixes without radically changing the whole system, as for example the endings *0/-(e)s* for the couple of singular/plural of the morphological category of number of the noun. The criterion is cited from Strang: "inflection involves relatively few variables in a closed system." (Strang, 1970:101) Bauer contends that "the general rule is that affixes which are members of large classes to which new items can be freely added are not inflectional; those which are members of small classes to which it is not possible to add extra members are inflectional." (Bauer, 1983:23) Cruse holds that inflectional affixes "change at a relatively slow rate through time, so that a single speaker is unlikely to see loss or gain of items in their lifetime" (Cruse, 2004:87), while the opposite seems true of derivational endings. Adams (1973) points to complementariness and mutual interdependence of members of a particular close set of items. Another dimension of this factor, suggested by the same author, is that it is a two-way relation, *ie* the existence of the 'unmarked' form is presupposed by the existence of the 'marked form' and *vice versa*. This property is observable only in relation to inflectional affixes. "With derived words, on the other hand, though the affixed form presupposes a base from which it was constructed, the reverse is not necessarily the case." (Adams, 1973:12)

The word *signature* in exx (1) and (2) is capable of being analysed into the morphs *sign* + *-at* + *-ure*. When the bound morph *-ure* is added (to the base *signat-*) the resulting item denotes a concrete result of the verbal action of *singing* (currently the verb *signate* is not quite frequently used in legal contexts to refer to the action of attaching one's signature) in (1) and several completed discrete acts of *signing* in (2). Other affixes that may possibly be ranked with this affix would be *-at/ion*, *-al*, *-ment*, *-ance* and also *-ing*:

(7) *There is no statutory prohibition against providing*[1236G] *for* ***hearings***[1237DN] *in chambers in the family cases;* (FD)

(8) *The* ***hearing***[1206DN] *of cases is divided into those which are heard in open court and those heard in chambers.* (FD)

As can be seen, the endings in neither the lists represent few variables in a closed system. Although the number of variables may be relative, the fact that the chance of including a new ending due to *eg* future borrowing remains open and, moreover, such inclusion would not disturb the system.

In sentence (3) the *-ing* ending stands as the sole formative so we cannot apply this test here. In ex (6) the *-ing* form functions as the main verb of a complex finite verb phrase conveying 'frame-time implications' as opposed to the simple finite verb form. In this case the ending may be ranked with the rest of verbal endings such as *0/-s/ed.* In exx (4) and (5) the simple *-ing* may be opposed to the perfect *have* + *-ed* in the perfect form of this construction. The status of the *-ing* affix in the last three examples may under this criterion be treated as inflectional as it forms a closed system that cannot be freely extended without being functionally disturbed. In exx (4) and (5) the *-ing* stands outside the regular verbal paradigm. What seems interesting is the fact that the *-ing* form is the 'unmarked' item as opposed to its perfect or passive counterpart, while with the regular verbal endings ex (6) it is the uninflected form that is usually considered as the 'unmarked' form.

4.2 Inflectional morphology is what is relevant to syntax

The second criterion concerns "substitutability within a syntagmatic frame. If a series of parallel word-forms are considered in isolation from their syntactic environment, and a given affix can be replaced by one or more other affixes wherever it occurs, then it can be said to be highly commutable within the word-form." (Bauer, 1983:23) It may be exemplified by the replaceability of *-s* ending with *0/-ing/-ed* in a series of isolated words such as: *call/calls/calling/called, cover/covers/covering/covered.* The examples that seem to fit this criterion are (6): *signs/sign/signing/signed* and also (4) and (5). The ending in ex (4) may be paralleled to *have/being* + *-ed* in the pairs contrasting simultaneity *vs* anteriority, *eg signing/having signed,* or active *vs* passive perspective, *eg signing/being signed, having signed/having been signed.* Similarly, the ending in (5) shows the same contrasts with *-ed.* Moreover, this type displays also aspectual contrasts progressive *vs* non-progressive, *eg having signed/having been signing* (at least in the perfect as its simple forms indicate progressiveness implicitly).

On the other hand, the counterparts of *-ure* which are used to form words that indicate the common meaning of 'result of verbal action' in ex (1), and "abstract nominalizations" (Bauer, 1983:221) in ex (2), such as *-al, -ion, -ment, -ance,* cannot be freely substituted for each other, *eg: signature/ signal*/ signation*/ signment*/ signance*, acquiture*/ acquittal/ acquittion*/ acquittment*/ acquittance**. Hence, it may be considered as demonstration of low commutability of endings within the word-form, *ie* the asterisked examples are defective. As demonstrated, the *-ing* forms exemplified in (4), (5) and (6) thus may be regarded as displaying a higher commutability within the word than the rest. Moreover, as can be seen, the range of the potential to indicate verbal morphological distinctions increases towards the ex (6).

The opposite of high commutability within the word form is the feature of low commutability on the sentential level as pertaining to the inflectional status as well: "in any given sentence, the possibility of commuting the affixes which are highly commutable within the word-form will tend to be low." (Bauer, 1983:24) "Inflection can be said to be characterized by high commutability within the word-form, but low commutability within the sentence." (Bazell, 1953:69, cited in Bauer, 1983:24) The test consists simply in trying to replace the ending with another item from the set to find out whether what results is a grammatical or ungrammatical sentence (the former would indicate derivation, the latter inflection).

In sentence (6) the *-ing* ending cannot be freely replaced by *0/-s/-ed* without leaving an ungrammatical sentence. The same applies to the sets of endings in (4) and (5):

(4) *The United States, which has signalled its intention to ratify by formally* ***signing (being signed*/ having signed?/having been signed*)*** *the Convention, now stands as the only industrialized country in the world and one of only two United Nations member states yet to make this legal commitment to children.* (Chromá, 2003:443)

(5) ***Having signed/signing?/being signed*/having been signed*/having been signing**** *the contract the party cannot revoke his/her offer without being subject to legal consequences.* (private instrument)

(6) *If there was an express agreement that the man who was* ***signing/sign*/signs*/signed**** *was not to be liable, the section would not apply.* (Chartrand, 1997:92)

Testing the exx (1) and (2) the following may be the result:

(1) *The Manager is authorised to bind the company with his sole signat**ure**, decis**ion**, judg**ment**...* (private instrument)

(2) *... total number of sign**atures** (acquitt**als**, amend**ments**, ratifi**cations**, hear**ings**...) not followed by ratifications:16; ...* (Chromá, 2003:443)

Although demonstrating a low commutability on the level of the lexeme, these endings show a high substitutability on the sentential level although, naturally, we have to consider the fact that the tested representatives would be derived from various bases.

Both the tests seem inapplicable in respect of the form in (3) as the ending of this form does not have any counterparting affixes whose addition would result in creating nominalisations conveying a similar degree of processuality and displaying analogical morpho-syntactic potential.

Another test suggested under this heading deals with the marking of agreement (of both types: *concord, ie* the compulsory marking of one grammatical category in two or three words to show their syntactic unity, and *government, ie* the compulsory expression of a certain element and marking of its particular form required by another sentence element). The universality of the holding that "Morphs whose form is specified by rules of agreement are inflectional" (Bauer, 1983:24) is subject to doubt by Bauer who points to the intricacy that not all endings which are traditionally considered as inflectional actually mark agreement. We do not find this criterion applicable to the *-ing* forms in question mainly for the latter reason.

As the above analysis shows, the tests suggest that the status of the forms exemplified in (1) and (2) may be treated as derivational while the status of the forms exemplified in (4), (5) and (6) may be considered as inflectional. Example (3) cannot be subject to this test as its ending stands as a sole formative in its class.

4.3 Derivational affixes are nearer the root than inflectional ones

The position of the ending is mentioned as the next criterion, *ie* inflection is marked further from the root. As the endings in all our examples are added directly to the root, (*ie* root=base/stem), with the exception of *-ure* added to base *signat/*, the test is irrelevant for our particular purpose.

4.4 Derivatives can be replaced by monomorphemic forms

The test of irreplaceability/replaceability of a word by a simple root form in a sentence bears inflectional implications for the former and derivational implications for the latter quality. Replacing the word *signature* with *sign* seems admissible although the latter would lack the semantic specification of the former:

(1) *The Manager is authorised to bind the company with his sole* ***signature/sign***. (private instrument)

As for the second example the word *signatures* may be substituted by the simplex *(completed) acts (of signing)*:

(2) *... total number of **signatures**/(completed) **acts** (of signing) not followed by ratifications:16; ...* (Chromá, 2003:443)

The third example may be replaced by the word *act(ion* of signing with agential implications):

(3) *However, even if a particular contract requires a writing, this does not mean that both parties must sign it or that the **signing/act(ion of signing)** occur at the time of contracting.* (Chromá, 2003:377)

The rest of the examples does not allow for their being replaced by simple root lexemes:

(4) *The United States, which has signalled its intention to ratify by formally **signing/sign*/act*** the Convention, now stands as the only industrialized country in the world and one of only two United Nations member states yet to make this legal commitment to children.* (Chromá, 2003:443)

(5) ***Having signed**/sign*/act* the contract the party cannot revoke his/her offer without being subject to legal consequences.* (private instrument)

(6) *If there was an express agreement that the man who was **signing/sign*/act*** was not to be liable, the section would not apply.* (Chartrand, 1997:92)

The conclusion therefore seems to be that by reference to this criterion the *-ing* endings in exx (1), (2) and (3) may be considered derivational while in the rest of the examples the inflectional nature of the affix is indicated.

4.5 Inflection is productive, derivation semi-productive
4.6 Inflectional affixes have a regular meaning

The two of the criteria may be treated in one paragraph as productivity is inherently connected with semantic predictability. Lack of gaps in the paradigm and semantic regularity are suggested as further factors accounting for the inflectional status of an ending, although Bauer points to the existence of gaps in paradigms of some of otherwise regular inflectional affixes on the one hand (lack of regular verbal inflectional affixes with modal verbs), and on the other hand, also to the semantic regularity of certain affixes that are normally treated as derivational (agentive *-er*, pacientive *-ee*).

The regularity in the paradigms may be ascertained in respect of the ending exemplified in (6), except for the impossibility to add it to modal and stative verbs. The same obtains also in respect of exx (4) and (5) except that their paradigms seem to be even more regular as they also include the stative verbs. Example (3) is restricted to processual verbs and the rules for adding the suffix *-ure* to verbal bases show a complementation pattern with the rest of the endings mentioned in the list.

Adams holds that "Affixes operating as inflections are stable in function and meaning. Plural *s* and past tense *ed* (or their variants) have the same significance whatever their context. This is often not the case with derivational affixes, ... (which may) have more than one meaning and can be added to more than one category of base words (*-able*: *allowable*= 'can be allowed', *companionable*= 'fitted to be, behaving like, a companion')" (Adams, 1973:12).

Semantic regularity cannot be found in respect of the ending in the first example as the words that can be ranked within this type may express various semantic implications (events, psychological concepts, concrete or abstract results of action, objects *etc.*) Similarly, in respect of the group represented by the second of our examples Bauer supplies the following semantic nuances associated with the verbal action identifiable, as we assume, only in a particular sentential context: 'act/state/process/place/countable result/uncountable result/something used in carrying out/system for carrying out', *etc.* (Bauer, 1983:185) What they share in common is, in our opinion, a certain degree of abstractness/conceptuality if compared with the following types. Derivational affixes "tend to be much less generalized in meaning than inflectional affixes." (Adams, 1973:13)

Semantic implications of the rest of the types seem to be quite regular. As for the third type its meaning is definitely that of the action taking place + processuality hand in hand with a certain degree of abstractness as opposed to that of the rest of the three forms. Its agentive implication is stronger than with the types exemplified in (1) and (2) but weaker than it is with the rests of the types. Examples (4) and (5) denote factitiveness/(potentially also manner with ex (4)) + agentive implication + processuality. The sixth example conveys, as mentioned before, 'frame time implications' again quite regularly (although this meaning of the expanded tenses, *ie* indication of "relatively longer duration in comparison with some other fact" (Jespersen, 1965d:179), is supposed to be fundamental for Jespersen, other semantic implications may be implied as well: "'terminate force' – the expanded form often represents the act as a whole, hence it has terminate force: 'I am sorry you doubt my statement. I *am telling* you the truth.' The common form, 'I *tell* you the truth,' could not be used here, for its meaning is so general that it is not felt as suitable for reference to this particular case." (Curme, 1980:206). For Leech (1971) the progressive aspect is usually used to refer to temporary happenings (indicating duration, limited duration or incompleteness of an action), repetition of events of limited duration, persistent or continuous activities.

From the semantic point of view, as suggested above, what we are facing here is, in our opinion, a scalar articulation of the verb-related meaning 'ACTION' with various degrees of abstractness /factitiveness /processuality/ agentive implication distributed among the respective types of *-ing* forms.

The tests presented in this section seem to justify the inflectional character of all the *-ing* forms except for those exemplified in (1) and (2) where the derivational status is supported again.

4.7 Derivation may cause a change of category

It is assumed that while inflectional affixes leave the categorical status of the stem untouched, derivational affixes do change the category of the base. This rule is contested by indefiniteness of the concept of category. "Categories are determined by distribution: if two items have identical distributions, they will be considered to belong to the same category. But it is not clear just how closely a distribution is to be defined." (Bauer, 2003:93) The categorial changes generally mean the changes of the word-class status *acquit>acquittal* (verb>noun) or the changes within the word-classes, *eg lion>lioness* (male>female), *boy>boyhood* (animate/concrete>inanimate/abstract), and they are treated as indicating the process of derivation. This substantial change has consequences for the shaping of the semantic, morphological and syntactic potential of the resulting form. "Any suffix which changes the syntactic class of a derivative must also change the syntactic classification of the derivative to fit in with the syntactic patterns ascribed to the new form class." (Bauer, 1983:180) It was pointed to already by Tesniére (1934) that the change of a syntactic function (verb to noun) results in the alteration of the syntactic character of the original verbal participants (*eg* adverbial modifier to adjective modifier).

This is specifically connected with our present problem. In the first three of our examples the affix is clearly derivational, *ie* it turns verbs to nouns (on the tests of the nominal status of *-ing* forms see Supplement Two pp. 1-2), although the third example shows also some verbal features (*eg* processuality, preservation of verbal valency: *the charging with theft versus the charge of theft*). As regards the last example, its status is quite certain, *ie* the resulting item is verbal, the form being employed aspectually.

The status of the ending in (4) and (5) is, however, not quite definite as the tests to be employed in order to determine whether a noun or a verb was formed would show that the resulting new items mix up the qualities of both word classes. Bauer suggests two possible approaches: either it must be admitted that inflection can change category (and we can assign inflectional status to the affixes in question) or there exists homophony of affixes (*ie* there are several distinct affixes, some of them are inflectional, the others are derivational).

4.8 Conclusion

To sum up, in the course of the present analysis we intentionally avoided explicit terms to refer to the exemplified forms so that we may not indicate their specific word-class assignment from the very beginning. The analysis might have contributed to the justification of distinct labels being used in respect of the presented types. We shall only repeat the terms here as they were introduced in the course of our previous deliberations:

1. deverbal nouns
2. non-*ing* verbal nouns
3. -*ing* verbal nouns
4. gerunds
5. participles (as sentence condensers)
6. participles (as main verbs of complex finite verb phrases)

As demonstrated, none of the above criteria (and their list is far from being complete) may alone serve as an indicator of inflectional/derivational nature of an ending. For readers' convenience we shall repeat the above criteria once more:

1. Inflection uses a closed set of affixes
2. Inflectional morphology is what is relevant to syntax
3. Derivational affixes are nearer the root than inflectional ones
4. Derivatives can be replaced by monomorphemic forms
5. Inflection is productive, derivation semi-productive
6. Inflectional affixes have a regular meaning
7. Derivation may cause a change of category

Table 1. should summarise the results of the above tests as they were employed in respect of the above six types of -*ing* forms.

Table 1. Testing inflectional *versus* derivational nature of the -*ing* ending in respective forms.

	DN	non-*ing* VN	-*ing* VN	G	P	Main V
Test1	derivation	derivation	-----------	inflection	inflection	inflection
Test2	derivation	derivation	-----------	inflection	inflection	inflection
Test3	derivation	derivation	derivation	inflection	inflection	inflection
Test4	derivation	derivation	derivation	inflection	inflection	inflection
Test5	derivation	derivation	inflection	inflection	inflection	inflection
Test6	derivation	derivation	inflection	inflection	inflection	inflection
Test7	derivation	derivation	derivation	derivation	derivation	inflection

DN – deverbal noun, VN – verbal noun, G – gerund, P – participle, V – verb

Bauer concludes his discussion of the topic in question by proposing two possible solutions: either to understand these criteria in terms of linguistic typology or to make a more delicate distinction within to concept of inflectionality, *ie* to distinguish between inherent inflection (that which is not inherently determined by the syntax) and contextual inflection (that which is determined by the syntactic structure) with the issue of *-ing* forms being solved in terms of the former.

The other solution derived from the conception of linguistic typology is based on the notion of a language prototype in Skalička's meaning: "an ideal model of mutually favourable language properties never fully realised in any natural language" (cited in Sgall, 1993:271, "typ jazyka jako ideální extrém (konstrukt) sestávající z navzájem si příznivých vlastností, ktorý není v plné míře uskutečnen v žádném jazyku.", translation: Janigová). With this approach the potentiality of language phenomena is conceptualised: "... a prototypical inflectional affix will not change major category, will have a regular meaning and will be added to every base in the appropriate part of speech; it will be ordered after all derivational markers, will be a member of a small closed set of affixes and will be relevant for the syntax in all models of syntax. A prototypical derivational affix will create new lexemes, change major category, have an irregular meaning on a fairly delicate analysis of meaning, especially in established words, come closer to the root than any inflectional affixes, belong to a large open set of affixes and will not play a role in the syntax of the sentence as a whole." (Bauer, 2003:107-106)

The *-ing* ending as a particular realisation of this prototypical potential of an affix in the English language may be considered in terms of growing multi-functionality of the affix, originally employed uniformly, that underwent the functional specification allowing for its current capability of being employed to indicate multiple semantic and morpho-syntactic potential of its realisations.

The following table should demonstrate the point. It comprises four action verbs (the first four items) and four stative verbs (the rest). In the category of deverbal and non-*ing* verbal nouns we omit the cases of conversion as these are usually interpreted as a distinct word-formation type.

Table 2. Multi-functionality of the *-ing* ending.

	DN	non-*ing* VN	*-ing* VN	G	P	Main V
to sign	signature	signature	signing	signing	signing	signing
to pass	passage	passage	passing	passing	passing	passing
to write	writing	writing	writing	writing	writing	writing
to draw	drawing	drawing	drawing	drawing	drawing	drawing
to own	ownership	ownership	---------	owning	owning	---------
to feel	feeling	----------	---------	feeling	feeling	---------
to be 'exist'	being	-----------	---------	being	being	---------
to have 'own'	----------	-----------	---------	having	having	---------

DN – deverbal noun, VN – verbal noun, G – gerund, P – participle, V – verb

The above table attempts to show the potential of the *-ing* ending to create a spectre of distinct forms which are distinguished as to their semantics, morphological and syntactic potential. It also shows that this ending serves as a gap-filler in the cases where none of the currently available affixes was employed to create the necessary form (it concerns deverbal nouns and non-*ing* verbal nouns). The gap-filling function of the *-ing* ending may be, and will be, demonstrated in the present thesis by examples on the combinability of respective types, where some *-ing* items function actually as non-*ing* deverbal nouns (they denote 'abstract action' or 'a single act' and they are factitive). One example may suffice at this place:

(9) *... a **borrowing** or **lending** of it (the thing) may amount to so treating it, but only if the **borrowing** or **lending** is for a period and in circumstances making it equivalent to an outright **taking** or **disposal**.* (TA)

Adams points to close relatedness of non-*ing* verbal nouns and *-ing* verbal nouns: "But a gerund which is followed by a prepositional phrase can be freely premodified: *his/the secret appointing of John,* and for the gerund here, which refers to the action itself, we can substitute a form with another (derivational) suffix, if there is one available: *'the secret appointment of John.'* Both *appointing* and *appointment* here may still mean 'the action of appointing,' but the latter word may also have the meaning of a completed activity, and too, the meaning of 'post', as in *John's appointment was a lucrative one.*" (Adams, 1973:24)

This interpretation seems to correspond with ours in its semantic aspect. Nevertheless, slight inconsistency may be noticed in that, on the one hand, Adams employs the term gerund to cover both types, *-ing* verbal nouns and gerunds in our classification, as if it were one unique type, and, on the other hand, she settles the issue of derivation *versus* inflection in respect of the *-ing* ending by contending that the last two items (namely, *appointment* and *appointing* as representing, in our classification, the types non-*ing* and *-ing* verbal nouns, respectively) are formed by derivational suffixes, while the *-ing* ending in the gerund that can be added to every verb and that shows the verbal potential attains the inflectional status, *ie* she actually admits that there exist two distinct types: *-ing* verbal nouns and gerunds.

Next, it may also be noticed that the gerundial and participial capacity of this ending is even more productive than its verbal capacity (only modals cannot stand to be bases for the gerund or participle) and that *-ing* verbal nouns are not formed from stative bases as their inherent semantic range is definitely processual slightly implying the idea of agent.

(10) *The signing of the treaty was deferred till the Lords Justices... should arrive.* (Oxford English Dictionary, 1989:461)

If the multifunctionality of the *-ing* ending were to be approached in terms of homophony it would mean to deny the common origin of the forms ending in *-ing* as well as the existence of rather delicate borderlines between some of their particular realisations. Rather than speaking of homophony we should prefer the concept a graded scale: on the one end of this scale there could be placed the *-ing* ending of deverbal nouns and non-*ing* verbal nouns and it may be assigned a derivational status, the opposite end of this scale would be represented by an inflectional nature of the *-ing* ending in respect of the participles functioning as main verbs in complex finite verb phrases. As for the *-ing* verbal nouns, gerunds and participles as condensers the status of the *-ing* ending may be treated as transient between derivation and inflection.

5. Status of respective types of *-ing* forms in terms of word-class assignment

As suggested above the hierarchy must inevitably be established among the criteria that may serve as a basis for the assignment of a particular word-class to a particular item. Its establishment will be unavoidably based on a subjective choice. We have already stated that our position is dominated by the functional view. From this perspective we find it necessary to start from the function that these forms may perform on the sentential level, the rest of the above criteria being subordinate to it (*ie* of persuasive rather than binding authority to put it legally). The core distinction between the function of nouns and verbs is that the former are primarily used to denote while the latter to predicate. If this is the maxim then, clearly, only deverbal nouns and non-*ing* verbal nouns denote an action (the change of syntactic category took place), while the rest of them serve to express predication, primary predication in the case of participles as main verbs of complex finite verb phrases and secondary predication in the case of *-ing* verbal nouns, gerunds and participles as sentence condensers (the change of syntactic category, as it were, did not occur). We distinguish between non-*ing* verbal nouns and *-ing* verbal nouns primarily for the reason that with the former the original verbal action was conceptualised to a larger extent than with the latter whose processuality and preservation of verbal valency is, in our opinion, still detectable.

As all the three forms (*-ing* verbal nouns, gerunds and participles) share this feature, *ie* the predicative property, with the verb many authors would treat them as verb forms. But the above analysis, hopefully, justified our position based on the contention that the *-ing* ending in these types of forms cannot be simply included in the list of verbal inflectional affixes. If we employ the above tests as supplementary to the criterion of function it can be hardly argued that these types are pure verbal forms as the ending in these cases does not belong to the closed set of verbal inflectional affixes. And although every verb (except for the modals) seems to be capable of being employed in the gerundial and participial capacity it is impossible to commute these forms within the sentential context of the participle functioning as main verb in a complex finite verb phrase and *vice versa.* Other arguments suggested before include the fact that gerunds and participles may be formed from stative verbs which even do not convey aspectual distinctions by means of a complex finite verb phrase with the main verb performed by the present participle. Moreover, gerunds may also be formed from nominal bases that do not have corresponding verbs at all. We assume that it is possible assert that these endings stand aside the regular verbal inflectional paradigm.

The closeness of these forms is perceivable on the semantic level. As mentioned before, they are united by the semantics of the original verb. What distinguishes them are various degrees of factitiveness, conceptuality, processuality and agentive implication (associated with the valency requirements of the original verb) manifested in individual types.

As regards the structural interpretation of constructions which are headed by the respective types, deverbal nouns, non-*ing* verbal nouns and *-ing* verbal nouns are deemed heads of noun phrases (the least regular of which seems to be the structural interpretation of the constructions headed by *-ing* verbal nouns which preserve verbal complementation pattern of the original verb in the cases where the original verb takes prepositional object *cf the charge of theft versus the charging with theft*). The structural interpretation of the participle in the function of the full verb is that of the main verb in a complex finite verb phrase. Gerunds and participles functioning as sentence condensers are treated as heads of semi-clause constructions (also referred to as non-finite clauses in the literature). We prefer the term semi-clause constructions as it seems to imply the gradient character of the structures headed by them more aptly. The common feature distinguishing them from the constructions conveying primary predication is the lack of independency, *ie* they can stand only as elements of finite clauses or they may be embedded in noun phrases or other semi-clause constructions.

The last mentioned-type deserves some attention as in the cases of gerundial embedding within another gerundial semi-clause the phrasal/purely nominal structural interpretation of the latter would assign the former a status of nominal participant. The inherent clause-like nature of the constructions headed by gerunds, however, justifies the assignment of a verbal participant status to the embedded gerundial semi-clause. To exemplify our point the following sentences may be supplied:

(1) *Subparagraph (1) above shall not apply to taking or* ***destroying fish by angling*** *in the daytime...* (TA)

(2) *... I would, by the application of the general principles of the law of contract, have little difficulty in* ***construing the notice requirements... as being of the essence.*** (CHD)

Should the first gerund be treated as a noun, the character of the construction headed by it would inevitably have to be phrasal and the other gerund would serve as a nominal postmodifier. On the contrary, if the first gerund is considered as an element that functions as semi-predicator, the structure is semi-clausal and then the second gerund in the construction must be considered as adverbial modifier in ex (1) and as prepositional object complement in ex (2). As the essential function of the gerund is to convey secondary predication, the latter interpretation seems to be more plausible (this is also the reason why these constructions are often referred to as *non-finite clauses*), as mentioned before.

The diachronic account might have made it clear that the very origin of these forms was nominal rather than verbal, but that they have gradually started to resemble the verb in their most important qualities although it cannot be asserted that they have fused with it completely.

The word-formation analysis showed that the *-ing* ending seems to be multifunctional – it may operate as pure derivational as well as pure inflectional affix while when it is employed to generate *-ing* verbal nouns, gerunds and participles its status is transitional between two of the kinds.

Yet, another dimension of gradience may be detected. It concerns interpretation of gerundial and participial constructions in certain syntactic functions: the adverbial syntactic function and the complementation patterns: activeV + O + as + *-ing*, and it passive variant: passiveV + as + *-ing*.

First, the adverbial syntactic function may be performed by the constructions that may be structurally interpreted as noun phrases, prepositional phrases, clauses and semi-clause constructions. Our attention is here obviously directed to the last mentioned type, *ie* gerundial and participial semi-clause constructions as adverbials. There exist general agreement among linguists in respect of the fact that distinction between the gerund and the participle seems to be obliterated in this particular syntactic function. Looking at the couples of the following examples we can see that the only material difference between them is whether the semi-clause construction complements a preposition or whether it follows a conjunction, *eg:*

(3) *...* ***in considering[630G] the application of section 31A*** *the court should ignore the terms of the new lease...* (CHD)

(4) *Later,* ***when considering***[431Part] ***section 31A and the argument whether the landlord could reasonably carry out the intended works without obtaining***[432G] ***possession of the holding***[433DN]*, the judge said...* (CHD)

(5) ***In reaching***[153G] ***such a conclusion*** *I am comforted that that view is entirely consistent with the conclusion of Browne-Wilkinson LJ in Mecca Leisure, ...* (CHD)

(6) *The judge returned to this* ***when setting***[415Part] ***out his overall conclusion on whether the intended works satisfied the first part of section 30(i)(f).*** (CHD)

(7) *... this would be a relevant factor* ***in deciding***[625G] ***whether those works could be carried out without obtaining***[626G] ***possession.*** (CHD)

(8) *... that in such cases,* ***when deciding***[666Part] ***whether section 31A applies,*** *(a) the court is not limited to...* (CHD)

(9) *Thus the issue of whether such a provision would be a sufficient "contraindication" to rebut the general presumption that time was not of the essence* ***in construing***[64G] ***such clauses*** *was not directly considered.* (CHD)

(10) *As Lord Reid said in Heath v Drown [1973] AC 498, 506* ***when construing***[344Part] ***the 1954 Act.*** (CHD)

The meaning of both types is the same, *ie* they convey accompanying circumstances with temporal implications. Representatives of both may be transformed into a finite adverbial subordinate clause: 'when/while + Subject + Verb + Object'. It may be therefore argued that the status of the prepositions which are capable of being complemented by semi-clause constructions is approximating that of conjunctions. Jespersen (1965e:141) contends that this class of prepositions differs from the "full" prepositions such as *during* (which itself once had a semi-clausal character, see Chapter Three, p. 117) that may be followed only by noun phrases:

(11) ***During the building of this bridge*** *a dispute arose.* (Jespersen, 1965e:141)
versus

(12) ***In/During* considering***[630G] *the application of section 31A) the court should ignore the terms of the new lease...* (CHD)

(13) *Later,* ***when/during* considering***[431Part] *section 31A and the argument whether the landlord could reasonably carry out the intended works without obtaining*[432G] *possession of the holding*[433DN]*, the judge said...* (CHD)

As will be demonstrated by the corpus analysis, the preposition *during* does not occur at all to introduce semi-clause constructions. In its stead the preposition *in* is employed and it is by far more frequent than for example conjunctions *when* and *while.*

Similarly, prepositions *with* and *without* are often treated as introducing clauses: "Clauses introduced by *with* and *without* often convey little more than a vague notion of accompanying circumstances." (CGEL, 1985:1124) Curme points to semantic analogy obtaining between the following absolute nominative constructions:

(14) ***The bridge across the chasm being only a single tree trunk****, we hesitated to attempt the passage.* (Curme, 1980:82)

(15) ***With knowledge increasing by leaps and bounds*** *we have reached a time when we must be content with specialisms.* (Curme, 1980:82)

The author uses the term *prepositional clause* which shows that the nature of a preposition may be close to that of a conjunction: "The preposition *with* is often placed before the absolute nominative construction, so that the expression in a formal sense becomes a prepositional clause but in spirit remains unchanged." (Curme, 1980:82)

Nevertheless, in the case of prepositional complementation realised by a semi-clause construction it is still possible to insert the agent of an *-ing* form in the possessive case. This seems inadmissible when the semi-clause construction is introduced by or without a conjunction in this function. In the present thesis we class the type that follows a preposition as gerundial while the other type following a conjunction or introduced without a conjunction as participial in this syntactic function admitting that both structures are very close to each other.

The second issue may be demonstrated by the following sentences:
Pattern: activeV/infinitive/gerund + O + as + -ing form

(16) *... the judge was wrong* ***to regard the decision*** *of Mecca Leisure Ltd v Renown Investments Ltd (1984) 49 P&CR 12* ***as binding***[15Part] ***on him****...* (CHD)

(17) *I would apply the presumption first* ***to construe clause 4(8) as not amounting***[124Part] ***to a deeming***[125G] ***provision...*** (CHD)

(18) *In Mecca Leisure, Eveleigh LJ simply* ***dismissed the decision in AWADA as being***[148Part] ***of "no help at all"*** *since it was decided on the wording*[149DN] *of the particular lease which was different from that in the case he was considering*[150V]. (CHD)

(19) *... when* ***he paraphrased the final words*** *of the paragraph 'without obtaining*[528G] *possession of the holding*[529DN]*'* ***as meaning***[530Part] ***'if a new tenancy is granted'***... (CHD)

Pattern: passive V/infinitive/gerund + as + -ing form

(20) *I think in the present case that the tile work which lines the wall, the wooden floorboards covered by a metallic surface which constitute the demised floor and the roller shutter which provides the enclosure of the fourth side of the shop are all* ***capable of being***[422G] ***described as having***[423Part] ***been constructed*** *or at least meaningfully of being*[424G] *demolished, ...* (CHD)

(21) *I think that section 46 lays down this principle generally, and that section 22, is, so far as publicity of hearing*[1180DN] *is concerned,* ***to be read as making***[1181Part] ***no exception in any class of suit or proceeding***[1182DN] ... (FD)

(22) *Interlocutory hearings*[1017DN] ***are not treated as being***[1018Part] ***determinative of civil rights...*** (FD)

(23) *There are situations outside the exceptions in section 12 which* ***have been long recognised as requiring***[1274Part] ***confidentiality***. (FD)

These complementation patterns show a somewhat obscure character as regards the status of the *-ing* forms which complement the preposition *as*. Quirk *et al.* (1985), (see Supplement Two, pp 41-42), treat the portion *as* + *-ing* of these patterns as being a prepositional complement of either the object (where the governing finite verb is active) or that of the subject (in the case of the passive finite verb). The verb valency in this pattern is complex transitive, the *as* + *-ing* complement being an obligatory element in these patterns. From the semantic point of view the *as* + *-ing* complement conveys a secondary predication related to the object (or subject in the passive variant: "in passive sentences the valency object becomes subject" (Allerton, 1982:109)).

Allerton (1982:110) who treats the verbs occurring in this pattern as trivalent (Valency Structure 124X in his classification as the subclass of Valency Structure 124 with a predicative introduced by a preposition *as*): SUBJECT + V + OBJECT + as-PREDICATIVE, with the as-PREDICATIVE section being an obligatory element allowing for commutability of nouns and adjectives (and in our case also *-ing* gerundial/participial forms).

Another interpretation of the section *as* + *-ing* in this pattern may be that of obligatory adverbial: V + Object + Adverbial/*as* + *-ing*: manner/comparison), *ie* the verb is trivalent taking an object plus a manner adverbial. In Allerton's classification that would be Valency Structure 127: SUBJECT + V + OBJECT + ADVERBIAL ELABORATOR:

(24) *Oliver treated Charles badly.* (Allerton, 1982: 113),

but the author does not provide the prepositional variant of this pattern. It is also Curme who treats this *as* + *-ing* element as adverbial of manner: "Manner is frequently expressed by a participle or a participial clause" (Curme, 1980:80):

(25) *Please do not understand me as having lost the hope.* (Curme, 1980:80)

The tests serving as the basic distinguishing criteria between the gerundial and participial interpretation of an *-ing* form seem to be mixed up together here: on the one hand, it is the gerundial capability of functioning as prepositional complementation, and, on the other hand, the possibility to paraphrase the as + *-ing* section by a relative clause (which is normally the participial property). As mentioned above the status of the preposition in connection with the *-ing* forms is resembling that of conjunction: "although as is classed as a preposition in the above pattern, it in some ways resembles the conjunction as which introduces clauses of comparison." (Quirk et al., 1985:1201) In the present analysis we decided to class the *-ing* forms occurring in this pattern as participial. This position is supported by the observation that it is impossible to insert the agent of the *-ing* action in the possessive case in this type of construction. This might be taken as another example of a rather vague borderline between two of the types in certain syntactic functions.

All of the above notes might have, hopefully, explained and justified the position which we defend in relation to the issue of *-ing* forms. The semantic, morpho-syntactic and structural account as well as the explication of their formation from both the diachronic and synchronic points of view might have accounted for a separate treatment of several distinct types of *-ing* forms conceived as items creating a cline from the full nominality towards the full verbality, *ie* some of them may be ranked with the word-class of nouns (deverbal nouns, non-*ing* verbal nouns), and verbs (participles as main verbs of complex finite verb phrases), while others represent various degrees of gradience between nouns and verbs (*-ing* verbal nouns, gerunds and participles). Moreover, the process of transition may be seen also in respect of *-ing* verbal noun>gerund, gerund>participle, participle>adjective/preposition/conjunction.

As the diachronic survey showed that all of these types may be associated with one common ending which has been gradually loaded up with a range of functions that have extended the scope of its original derivational nature, we assume that this phenomenon may serve as an example of language dynamism in action. It testifies of the language potential to re-interpret the inventory of its existing means in accordance with its current communicational aims. The above account might have also shown how substantial may be the impact of the function of a language unit on its form.

CHAPTER TWO
Corpus analysis

1. Corpus characteristics

Actual realisations of the phenomenon under review were studied in the corpus of legal English. We expected that the texts used in legal settings would provide a broad empirical ground for the study of *-ing* forms as they seemed to abound in versatile representatives of the *-ing* spectre that was in the centre of our research attention. Before proceeding to characterise the analysed corpus the term *legal English* needs some comments.

The topic of legal English has attracted the attention of social scientists, sociolinguists, linguists as well as lawyers since 1970s, the research booming especially in the United States, Israel, Britain, Sweden and the former West Germany. It might be argued that it developed into a new inter-disciplinary branch of humanity sciences (sometimes referred to as *jurilinguistics*) due to the special nature of the relationship between law and language. It is generally agreed that the law is essentially dependent on the language: "Language is medium, process and product in the various arena of the law where legal texts, spoken or written, are generated in the service of regulating social behaviour." (Maley, 1994:11), "Words are obviously of paramount importance in the law; in a most basic sense, the law would not exist without language." (Danet, 1980:448), "it (legal language) is the primary *tool* of the legal professional" (Charrow *et al.*, 1982: 180).

There are various variants of the term legal English employed more or less interchangeably: *legal language* (Danet, 1985, Bhatia 1993, Charrow *et al,* 1982, Crystal and Davy, 1969), *the language used in legal discourse* (Trosborg, 1992), *language of the law*, *law language* (Bhatia, 1993, Mellinkoff, 1963), *legal sublanguage* as one of professional sublanguages/*legal language* (Charrow *et al.*, 1982).

Kurzon (1989) attempts to distinguish between the terms *legal language* and *language of the law* by reserving the latter for "the language or the style used (or the sublanguage used) in documents that lay down the law, in a very broad sense... legislation, and also documents pertaining to private law such as contracts, wills, deeds, since they in their own way lay down the law for the people involved." (Kurzon, 1989:283-284) On the other hand, the term *legal language* should be used to denote "the language used when people talk about the law. This is the language that is used in legal textbooks, lawyers speech and in their correspondence. It is also used by judges when giving their decisions." (Kurzon, 1989:284). Kurzon often refers to this type as *metalanguage.*

Trosborg (1992) treats the *language of the law* (legislation and private instruments) as a hyponym of a general, superordinate term *legal language*. This common umbrella term includes also language of the courtroom, language in textbooks, lawyers' speech and people thinking about law.

For the present purposes, the term *legal language* (*ie legal English*) will be used as a general term to be employed wherever language is used for communicative purposes associated with the subject matter of law.

To denote various final products of the employment of legal language for a particular communicative purpose in a particular communicative situation there are again available several terms: *genres or types of language use in legal settings/registers* (Danet, 1980), *genres* (Bhatia, 1993), *text types* (Kurzon, 1989), *legal discourse types/ use-based styles/registers/genres* (Maley, 1987), *sub-languages of legal language* (Trosborg, 1991), *stylistic layers of legal language* (Tomášek, 1998, Vystrčilová, 2001).

We can agree with Maley in that "discourse types or genres characteristically organise their content, message, within broadly recognisable structural shapes; that is to say, we can categorise the texts that are the products of the discourse process according to the configuration of structural elements that they exhibit." (Maley, 1994:18) Thus every discourse type has a distinct internal organisation or structure. However, Maley sometimes uses also the term *register* as an equivalent of a genre or discourse type. In Bolinger's conception: "A *register* is a variety that is not typically identified with any particular speech community but is tied to the communicative occasion. ... it is a question of various degrees of formality." (Bolinger, 1975:358). In our research the terms *types of legal discourse* or *genres* are used interchangeably and the concept of *register* is used in Bolinger's meaning.

Various criteria may be employed to specify distinct types of legal discourse. As Bathia puts it: "Legal language encompasses several usefully distinguishable genres depending upon the communicative purposes they tend to fulfil, the settings or contexts in which they are used, the communicative events or activities they are associated with, the social or professional relationship between the participants taking part in such activities or events, the background knowledge that such participants bring to the situation in which that particular event is embedded and a number of other factors." (Bhatia, 1993:101).

Danet's model of the legal language discourse typology (Danet, 1980:471) takes into account the formality of style, *ie register* in Bolinger's conception, and the form of media used (written or spoken). The scale of stylistic formality represents a cline ranging from formality to informality: frozen, formal, consultative, casual, and intimate. The author cross-classifies genres of legal language according to the register and medium used (written and spoken: composed and spontaneous):

a) frozen written: insurance policies, contracts, leases, wills
b) frozen spoken-composed: marriage ceremonies, indictments, witnesses' oaths, verdicts

c) formal written: statutes, briefs, appellate opinions
d) formal spoken-composed: lawyers' examination of witnesses in trials, lawyers motions
e) consultative spoken composed: lay witnesses' testimony
f) consultative spoken-spontaneous: lawyer-client interaction, bench conferences
g) casual spoken spontaneous: lobby conferences, lawyer-lawyer conversations (Danet, 1980:471).

Tomášek (1998) sets out a particular communicative situation, its subject-matter and participants to be the main criterion for his classification of stylistic layers of legal language:

a) legislative
b) application of law
c) jurisprudence
d) legal rhetoric
e) teaching law
f) mass-media
g) non-literate forms (slang, argot).

For Maley (1994) the primary criterion for the classification of legal discourse types is a discourse situation:

a) sources of law and originating points of legal process (legislature, regulations, by-laws, precedents, wills, contracts *etc*) – *written texts*
b) pre-trial processes (police/video interview, pleadings, consultations, subpoena, jury summons) – *spoken and written texts*
c) trial processes (court proceedings examination, cross-examination, intervention, rules and procedures, jury summation, decision) – *spoken texts*
d) recording of judgment in law reports (case reports) – *written texts.*

Many authors point to the fact that it is not possible to give a solid account of legal language in general, primarily for its multiple stratification and special characteristics pertaining to each type: "Only with the specification of sub-domains can we begin to look for characteristics specific to a particular legal sub-language." (Trosborg, 1991:67) The research into substantial features characterising a particular genre of legal language was primarily concentrating on the lexis, with growing interest in syntactic issues and text analysis. Since late 60s these aspects of legal language have been studied also in the light of the *theory of speech acts,* originally put forward by J.L. Austin (1962), as indicators of specific types of illocutionary functions to be effected by a particular legal discourse. The basic tenets of this theory centre around the classification of three aspects of every utterance: locution (sound and structure), illocution (communicative function) and perlocution (impact on the addressee). The original Austin's classification of illocutionary forces (verdictive, exercitive, commissive, behabitive and expositive) was later re-elaborated by his successors who advanced his notes, which concentrated mainly on linguistic features of performatives, by focusing on felicity conditions of a particular type of speech act, communicative principles, *etc.*

The corpus which we analysed in the past five years is composed of two distinct genres or discourse types of legal English, namely statutes and law reports of the English legal system. Here is the summary of their most conspicuous features as found in the literature.

Legislative discourse. The term *statute* is generally used to denote a particular outcome of legislative activities of the principal legislative body *ie* Parliament – it becomes a part of the source of law known as *primary legislation* or *statutory law*. Beside statutory law, which occupies, *de jure,* the second highest position in the hierarchy of the sources of English law (with the European Union law on the top), it is also delegated or subordinate legislation (*ie* statutory instruments, by-laws) that is ranked with legislation as the source of law: "legislation... is the largest and most powerful source of law in a society." (Maley, 1994:17) In England, ancient statutes were drafted and preserved as Statutes Rolls (1278-1468) by "judges, counsellors and officials... in Latin and Norman French." (Craies, 1971:21) From 1487 Latin and Norman French was replaced by English and drafting was handed over to a special category of lawyers – "conveyancers who were encouraged to prolixity by the invention of printing, and diluted their native language by that cautious use of synonyms which is the common characteristics of deeds and statutes." (Craies, 1971:22).

As to the position of a drafter of a statute, it is considered to be special in that the writer is not the original author of the text – the actual creator of the text is Parliament. Similarly, the addressee or the audience of the statute is public at large, but they actually perceive the wording of the statute through interpretation by lawyers and judges as intermediaries.

Regarding the drafting of legislative writing it is said to have "a long and well-established tradition... the style of legal documents has become firmly standardized, with the inevitable result that legal draftsmen tend to become comfortable with tried, tested and time-honoured linguistic expressions and style of writing over a period of time." (Bhatia, 1993:117) This may account for its formal character although not as formulaic or frozen as that of legal instruments such as deeds, contracts, wills *etc.* The style is also "highly impersonal, decontextualized... defining the(ir) model world of obligations and rights, permissions and prohibitions as precisely, clearly and unambiguously as linguistic resources permit" (Bhatia, 1993:102). On the other hand, Bhatia also points to 'all-inclusiveness' or explicitness of legislative provisions, the feature which is in contrast with the former. It is necessitated by a demand to cover every possible situation, eventuality or condition that might occur.

The structure of a modern English statute is rather uniform: long title, year and number, short title (sometimes placed at the end of the statute), preamble, enacting formula, body of the statute (further sub-divided into sequences), schedules.

Among the syntactic and stylistic features considered as characteristic of this genre, the following were mentioned in the literature: considerable frequency of complex prepositional phrases, binomial and multinomial expressions, syntactic discontinuities (insertion of qualifications next to the head to avoid ambiguity), repetition rather than pronominal reference as cohesive device, multiple negatives, subordinate clause embeddings, whiz-deletion, complex conditionals, precise textual articulation into parts/divisions, sections, subsections, paragraphs and sub-paragraphs with corresponding numbering, lettering and indexing with "a strong preference for a single sentence section or subsection," (Maley, 1987:39) and consequent production of long sentences with complex subordination and coordination, nominal character *ie* condensation of clauses to various types of nominalisations: Maley suggests that nominalisations not always result in condensation: "sentences using the nominal style are wordier than the corresponding verbal style... (however) nominalisations objectify the process and make it possible to be treated as something which is apart from persons and time, and which is a part of or a step in legal procedure. As nounlike elements in the sentence, they are more movable than verbs and can be placed in subject position and given thematic prominence." (Maley, 1987:40), the prominence of passive constructions, complex conditionals, high incidence of prepositional phrases, unusual length of sentences: "50 words per sentence is more or less the average" (Kurzon, 1989:285), textual mapping, *ie* "reference made to information found in other sections of the statute" (Maley, 1994:25), deeming sections as a kind of legal fiction, *etc*.

As for the nominal character of sentences, Crystal and Davy suggest that "one of the most striking characteristics of written Legal English is that it is so highly nominal, that is, many features in any given stretch are operating within nominal group structure, and the long complicated nominals that result are noticeable by contrast with the verbal groups, which are relatively few, and selected from a restricted set of possibilities." (Crystal and Davy, 1969:205) Similarly, our previous research into *-ing* forms in the genre of legislation showed that "In the style of a legislative legal norm of the analysed texts, we found preference for the use of prepositional phrases complemented by gerundial semi-clause constructions and verbal noun phrases to participial semi-clause constructions occurring after or without conjunctions in adverbial functions." (Janigová, unpublished PhDr-thesis, 214)

Studies deriving their approach from the Speech Acts Theory view the statute as "a rule-enacting document, ... its promulgation by the legislature is a speech act with illocutionary force of enacting." (Kurzon, 1986:9) From this perspective the most important part is the enacting formula deemed as an explicit exercitive performative (it contains the explicit performative verb *to enact* in a unique form of passive imperative *be* it *enacted* in the beginning of each statute) which determines the overall type of speech act the statute should effect and also serves as 'a master speech act' (Fotion, 1971:234), controlling the performative nature of the speech act status of every particular section of the statute (prohibiting, permitting, ordering...). Another interesting aspect is the anticipatory *it* as the grammatical subject of the passive verb, the real subject being the whole extraposed wording of the statute.

So it may be concluded that there are two tendencies working in legislative drafting: "generality, vagueness, syntactic condensation are, on the one hand, modes of organisation within the style which provide for flexibility; on the other hand, explicitness, specificity, technicality move in the direction of certainty and stability." (Maley, 1987:46), with the aim for legislative drafters to achieve equilibrium between the flexibility and certainty imperatives.

The Acts of Parliament Corpus consists of the wordig of the Theft Act 1968 and the Family Law Act 1996, the total of words being 51769.

Law Reports.

In England, judicial decisions of prominent importance are published in the form of official Law Reports serving as "authentic records of past judgments... taken as faithful records of all the facts of the case, the arguments of the judge, his reasoning, the judgment he arrives at and the way he does it, the kind of authority and evidence he uses and the way he distinguishes the present case from others cited as evidence either by him or by the opposing lawyers." (Bhatia: 1993:119) The importance of law reporting is due to the doctrine of *stare decisis* operating in the common law system. It states that: "every court is bound to follow any case decided by a court above it in the hierarchy, and appellate courts (other than the House of Lords) are bound by their previous decisions." (Cross, 1968:35) 'Intertextuality' is an important element. Every judicial formulation is always based on the relationship to a previous one in an earlier case or a potential future case: "(it) is the basic facilitating concept of the common law legal system" (Maley, 1994:47), and its is the essence of the doctrine of precedent.

Regular law reporting started with the Year Books, transcribed from the Plea Rolls begun in 1189 by apprentices to the law in Anglo-Norman. The Year Books published annually between 1283 and 1535 were superseded by personalised reports *ie* reports written privately by lawyers (*eg* Chief Justice Coke). English started to replace Latin in these documents in the 14th century:

"... it is at this very period, in 1362, that the Statute of Pleading establishes English as the language of the courts, and in the same year that Parliament was opened in English for the first time." (Strang, 1970:219) According to Maley: "It was not until 1650, by *An Act for Turning the Books of Law, and all Processes and Proceedings in Courts of Justice into English. 455, 1650, 11 Acts and Ordinances of the Interregnum* that English became the official language of the law." (Maley, 1994:12)

The tradition continued in the course of centuries until 1865 when the Incorporated Council of Law Reporting was established to publish authorised law reports titled *The Law Reports*. These are reports of important cases selected by the Council, written by lawyers, and approved by the judges involved. Today the Council also publishes *the Weekly Law Reports* and other important legal materials.

In each case in appellate proceedings there may be delivered as many as five full judgments comprising the summary of the facts of the case, explicit account of the reasoning that led a judge to the decision (here the *ratio decidendi* /that may become a part of case law/ and *obiter dicta* are usually distinguished) and the decision in the instant case.

Bhatia states the following structure of a law report:

1) Identifying the case
2) Establishing facts of the case
3) Arguing the case:
   (a) Stating history of the case
   (b) Presenting arguments
   (c) Deriving ratio decidendi
4) Pronouncing judgment. (Bhatia, 1993:135-136)

For Tomášek judicial decisions should be placed under the stylistic layer of application of law aimed to administer law – to bring it to life in the process of its application, mainly in judicial practice. The basic subtypes of legal discourse of this layer are judicial decisions and various kinds of decisions of state bodies. This stylistic norm, according to Tomášek, "is more relaxed with a tendency to customary selection of various language means, words as well as the whole collocations", (Tomášek, 1998:28, "Stylová norma už je volnější a přibližuje se spíše zvykovému užívání nejruznějších jazykových prostředku, slov i celých slovních spojení." Transl. Janigová)

Maley (1994) ranks Law Reports with the written judicial discourse type. Decisions in appellate proceedings of superior courts become a part of case law in the common law system: "The judgments of the higher appellate courts, in particular, represent the substance of the common law." (Maley, 1994:42) Maley points to the fact that the special position of the English judiciary influences also the style of this type of legal discourse if compared with its continental counterpart: "Continental judges are likely to be officials and bureaucrats: their decision-making is correspondingly restrained and frequently rigid in style and format. In the common law tradition, judges have been trained as advocates and their training has focused on the construction and balancing argument..." (Maley, 1994:42).

"The individual tenor of judgments" (Maley, 1994:43) is a typical feature of the styles of the written appellate judgments. The judgment is written in first person and its reasoning and speculation abounds in different forms of modality. A law report usually comprises several judgments of the judges who constituted the appellate bench of which only the opinion of the first judge is considered the judgment of the court, the rest either concurring or giving minority opinions.

The style of the judge's language is formal: "what distinguishes it from other types of formal language is basically the vocabulary." (Kurzon, 1986:58) The specific terminology is a striking feature of a legal discourse in general. Definitions of the terms of English legalese are products of judicial interpretation. The frequently cited enumeration of lexical specifics of legal English is that of Mellinkoff (1963:11): frequent use common words with uncommon meanings, frequent use of Old English and Middle English words, frequent use of Latin words and phrases, use of Old French and Anglo-Norman words which have not been taken into the general vocabulary, use of terms of art, frequent use of formal words, deliberate use of words and expressions with flexible meaning *etc.*

From the perspective of the Speech Acts Theory, Kurzon (1986) distinguishes two illocutionary forces of the judgment: on the one hand, the judge states the law for a particular case by reference to a statute or common law, and, on the other hand, the judge states the *ratio decidendi* rule which will become the source of law for future cases with analogical essential elements provided that all the felicity conditions required for this speech act are satisfied. Both of these have the linguistic form and pragmatic force of expressing opinion/declaring law. Their *de jure* effect is, however, that of law-making *ie* the whole judgment is binding on the instant case, and its *ratio decidendi* is binding on the grounds of the operation of the *stare decisis* doctrine on all future cases with similar facts.

The present corpus consists of the texts of 2 judgments of the Chancery Division and 1 judgment of the Family Division of the High Court (England) comprised in the Law Reports (Parts 11 and 12), published by the Incorporated Council of Law Reporting for England and Wales in 2002, the total of words being 51614.

2. Description of the method employed

The method of syntactic analysis has been the following: every *-ing* form will be detected, numbered and classified as either deverbal noun, verbal noun, gerund, participle, verb (main verb or auxiliary) or other word class which it can be ranked with due to the shift of syntactic function (*ie* adjectives, prepositions, conjunctions).

Verbal nouns, gerunds and participles will be then analysed in respect of structure. Verbal nouns function are constitutents of noun phrases whereas gerunds and participles are constituents of semi-clause constructions. All of them function as heads of these structures (the term ***head*** is understood here as "the obligatory element… which may function in a manner equivalent to the whole construction of which it is a part". (CGEL, 1985:61) When gerunds and participles function as premodifiers they become constituents of noun phrases.

The *-ing* forms with full verbal nature may operate as 'main verbs' (CGEL, 1985:61) of finite verb phrases functioning as the verb element of a clause or sentence structure or as auxiliaries indicating the progressive aspect of the passive or heads of infinitive semi-clause constructions in the progressive. As these three types of functions of *-ing* forms are beyond the scope of the present analysis they will only be identified and their occurrence will be indicated.

Finally the whole structures of which verbal nouns, gerunds and participles are constituents will be classified in respect of syntactic functions.

The process of embedding constituents of the same level of structural hierarchy is denoted by the signs in the following order: ____________, (), [].

The order of categories will be as follows:

VN/G/P – head of a NP/SemiCl, NP/SemiCl – PrepComp/syntactic function, PrepP – syntactic function, *eg:* the phrase:

a ground for refusing a licence will be structurally and syntactically analysed as follows:

> *[a ground (for <u>refusing a licence</u>)]: G – head of a SemiCl, SemiCl – PrepComp, PrepP – Postmod in a NP.*

3. Repertory of syntactic functions of gerundial and participial semi-clause constructions.

In the following section we shall comment on the repertory of syntactic functions performed by the gerundial and participial semi-clause constructions.

Quirk *et al.* reserve the term syntactic function for "the unit's privilege of occurrence, in terms of its positions, mobility, optionality, *etc*, in the unit of which it is a constituent." (CGEL, 1985:48) They include *determination*, *modification* and *complementation*.

The term *determination* is used for the function of words and (sometimes) phrases which, in general, determine what kind of reference a noun phrase has (definite, indefinite, universal, partitive). The items realising this function are referred to as determiners and they occur before the noun acting as the head of the noun phrase and before its premodifiers. Quirk *et al.* (1985) distinguish three classes of determiners:

* predeterminers, eg: half, all, double;
* central determiners, eg: the, a/an, some, any, no;
* postdeterminers, *eg:* cardinal and ordinal numerals, *many, few*.

Modification is, unlike *determination,* largely an optional function performed for instance by adjectives and by intensifying adverbs in the adverb phrase. The authors distinguish between *premodifiers,* which precede the head, and *postmodifiers,* which follow the head. Semantically, *modifiers* add a descriptive information to the head. The authors recognise the operation of *modification* only on the phrasal level, hence, the performance of this function by a clause does not attribute a multiple status to the whole sentence the noun phrase of which it modifies.

The term *complementation* is reserved for "the function of a part of a phrase or clause which follows a word, and completes the specification of a meaning relationship which that word implies." (CGEL 1995:65) The authors recognise the complementation of nouns, adjectives, adverbs or prepositions. "The distinction between *complementation* and *valency* consists in the inclusion of the subject in the case of *valency*, whereas *complementation* excludes it." (Dušková, 1999b:98). (For Quirk *et al. valency* is "the way in which a verb determines the kinds and number of elements that can accompany it in the clause." (CGEL, 1995:1169)). *Complementation* also occurs on the level of clause structure where complementation of the verb is performed by the object, complement and adverbial.

There are four types of verb *complementation* (Dušková, 1999b:98), namely *copular* (1), *monotransitive* (2), *complex transitive* (3) and *ditransitive* (4), *eg*:

(1) *John is only a boy.* – SVCs (Dušková, 1999:98b)

(2) *They like the children's visits.* – SVO (CGEL, 1985:1185)

(3) *She called him a hero.* – SVOCo (Dušková, 1999:98)

(4) *They asked the children a question.* – SVOO (CGEL, 1985:1186)

The terms *complementation* and *complement* are not used interchangeably in CGEL. While the former is used with a wide, universal scope of meaning as defined above, the latter is one of its manifestations, referring to a specific sentence element: "Complement is in a copular relationship with another clause element. The subject complement relates to the subject, and the verb is copular" (CGEL, 1985:728), *eg:*

(5) *They are very pleasant.* (CGEL, 1985:728) – sentence pattern SVCs

"The object complement relates to the direct object..." (CGEL, 1985:728), *eg*:

(6) *We find them very pleasant.* (CGEL, 1985:728) – sentence pattern SVOCo

"The object complement becomes the subject complement in the passive clause." (CGEL, 1985:729), *eg:*

(7) *His friends call him **Ted**[Object complement]*. (CGEL, 1985:729)

(8) *He is called **Ted**[Subject complement]*. (CGEL, 1985:729)

A note should be made on the discrepancy concerning the English terms 'subject and object complements' and the Slovak terms 'doplnok podmetu' and 'doplnok predmetu' that are only seemingly corresponding if we resort to word for word translation. Here follows the labeling of the syntactic functions in question in accordance with the English and Slovak terminological registers:

(9) *He was **sober**.* (Dušková, 1999b:100) – subject complement *Bol **triezvy**.* (Transl. Janigová) – menná časť verbo-nominálneho prísudku, *ie* 'nominal part of a verbonominal predicate' (transl. Janigová)

(10) *The jury found the defendant **guilty**.* (Janigová, Vargová 2001:148) – object complement
*Porota uznala obžalovaného **za vinného**.* (transl. Janigová) – predmet, *ie.* 'object in Slovak terminology'

(11) *The defendant was found **guilty**.* (Janigová, Vargová, 2001:152) – subject complement
*Obžalovaný bol uznaný **za vinného**.* (transl. Janigová) – predmet *ie.* 'object in Slovak terminology'

(12) *He came home **sober**.* (Dušková, 1999b:101) – optional predicative adjunct

Prišiel domov ***triezvy***. (transl. Janigová) – doplnok podmetu *ie*. 'subject complement in Slovak terminology'

(13) *They brought him home* ***drunk***. (Dušková, 1999b:101) – optional predicative adjunct
Priniesli ho domov ***opitého***. (Transl. Janigová) – doplnok predmetu *ie*. 'object complement in Slovak terminology'

Dušková summarises that "there are three elements to be distinguished, whatever names they may be given: an obligatory clause element complementing a copula (9), an obligatory subject or object complement due to the semantic structure of a full verb (10, 11), and an optional element qualifying the subject or the object in the course of verbal action (12, 13)." (Dušková, 1999b:103) In the present study we shall employ the terminology that is generally used in English grammar as presented above *ie* the term 'subject complement' for the syntactic function exemplified in (9), (11), the term 'object complement' for the function exemplified in (10), and the term 'subject or object predicative adjunct' for the syntactic function exemplified in (12), (13) and (14) below.

(14) *I saw Pam* ***going home***[*subject or object predicative adjunct*]. (CGEL, 1985:1126)

As for the function of object complement, it is generally agreed that *-ing* semi-clause constructions do not perform this function: "Object complements do not include finite or non-finite nominal clauses. Only nominalizations with the structure of noun phrases (having *wh*-words, derived nominals or gerundives as heads) can function as object complements." (Colen, 1984:19) In our PhDr-thesis we found one type of the *-ing* semi-clause construction which we interpreted in accordance with Quirk *et al.* as 'prepositional object complement' after the preposition *as*: "The preposition *as* designates a copular relation, particularly in specifying a role or status associated with the direct object. Following a complex transitive verb and a direct object, the prepositional complement of *as* functions semantically as an attribute, and may be termed a 'prepositional object complement'." (CGEL, 1985:1200) The repertory of verbs that occur in this construction includes: *accept as, acknowledge as, class as, define as, describe as , intend as, regard as, see as, treat as, etc* where the *as* preposition is obligatory, and *appoint (as), consider (as), deem (as), reckon (as), report (as), etc* where the as preposition is optional:

(15) *... on the application of a person entitled to recover from the person convicted any other goods directly or indirectly representing the first-mentioned goods as being the proceeds of any disposal or realization of the*

whole or part of them or of goods so representing them, the court may order those other goods to be delivered or transferred to the applicant; representing the first mentioned goods (as being the proceeds of any disposal... of goods so representing them): Participle – head of SemiCl, SemiCl – PrepComp, PrepP – PrepCo (TA)

In the present study we applied the criterion according to which *-ing* forms governed by a preposition were ranked with gerunds. Nevertheless, in the case of the *-ing* forms governed by the preposition *as* following the above repertory of verbs whose meaning requires obligatory complement attributing a quality or feature to either the subject or the object, we had to admit that these *-ing* forms should be classed with participles rather than gerunds despite the fact that they were governed by a preposition as they may be paraphrased by a relative clause, *eg representing the first mentioned goods as goods that are the proceeds of any disposal...*

The crucial function on the clausal level is, undoubtedly, that of attributing a quality or assertion to the subject of the clause, which is traditionally referred to as *predication.* The syntactic function of *predication* is realised by the *predicate* as one of the constitutive elements of the clause structure. In this respect, there is again terminological discrepancy as to the use of the term *predicate* and *predication* in English grammar (CGEL) and Slovak/Czech grammar. Quirk *et al.* use the term *predicate* to denote "that part of a statement which is asserted about the subject" (CGEL, 1985:79), and they use the term *predication* to denote that part of the *predicate* which is other than the *operator, ie* the first or only auxiliary in the verb phrase realising the sentence element Verb. "What Czech grammar terms the *predicate* in English grammar corresponds to the sentence element *Verb.*" (Dušková, 1999b:98) We shall use the English terminology.

Thus, in respect of the syntactic functions the elements of clause structure include: subject, verb, object, subject and object complement, modifiers, optional predicative adjuncts corresponding to the term *doplnok* in Slovak grammar.

In the following section we have attempted to exemplify respective syntactic functions carried out by the gerundial and participial semi-clause constructions. The syntactic functions are tabulated and the results summarised at the end of this section.

Gerundial and participial semi-clause constructions as modifiers

Both gerundial and participial semi-clause constructions may also function as modifiers within noun phrases. As has been suggested, there are two kinds of modifiers, namely postmodifiers and premodifiers. Before providing a sample of examples of both kinds let us supply their brief characteristics.

First of all we have to admit that due to the progress of adjectivisation we distinguish between *-ing* forms functioning as modifiers which have acquired the full adjectival status and so they may be ranked with the word class of adjectives, and those *-ing* forms which have not been converted into full adjectives yet.

The criteria for the full adjectival status are the following:
***** *the possibility of gradation***

(16) *a most astonishing piece of news* (Dušková, 1988:581)

***** *the possibility of intensification by very***

(17) *a very becoming dress* (Dušková, 1988:581)

***** *the admissibility of a copular verb other than to be***

(18) *This play seems amusing.* (Dušková, 1988:271)

The separation of fully adjectivised *-ing* forms from gerunds and participles may also be demonstrated by the shift of the valency (Dušková, 1988:271):

(19) *an amusing play* – intransitive *vs*
to amuse someone – transitive (Dušková, 1988:271).

Trnka (1956) further suggests that the adjective nature of an *-ing* form is obvious when it enters into word-formation processes *eg* prefixation (*unforgiving, outstanding*), composition (*pleasure-seeking, easy-going*), suffixation (*cunningly, exceedingly*).

On the other hand, the *-ing* forms which do not allow of gradation, cannot be premodified by the intensifying adverb *very,* and realise nominal predications with the copula *to be*, are deemed to have preserved their verbal character.

Gerundial and participial semi-clause constructions functioning as premodifiers are different in semantic and intonation respect. Curme points to "the adjective force and weaker stress," (Curme,1980a:215), of participial premodifiers. According to Dušková, gerundial *-ing* forms as premodifiers form with the constituent they modify one unit with falling intonation and the main stress on the first member and the secondary stress on the other member. These modifiers may be semantically paraphrased by prepositional postmodification (Dušková, 1988:269), *eg:*

(20) *melting point* (Dušková, 1988:269) – the point of melting.

Noun phrases with participial *-ing* forms as premodifiers show the level stress pattern and these constructions correspond to relative clauses (Dušková, 1988:269), *eg:*

(21) M*elting snow* (Dušková, 1988:269) – the snow that is melting.

As far as postmodification is concerned, it is obligatory when the *-ing* form is complemented by an object or adverbial and with the gerundial *-ing* forms it occurs after prepositions.

Neither *-ing* premodifiers, nor postmodifiers, may occur in the perfect aspect. "The perfective aspect cannot usually be expressed in the (postmodifying) nonfinite clause". (CGEL, 1985:1264)

(22) *The man who has won the race is my brother.* (CGEL, 1985:1264)

(23) *The man having won the race is my brother.** (CGEL, 1985:1264)

(24) *the firm that has built the bridge across the valley* (Dušková, 1988:272)

(25) *the firm having built the bridge across the valley* * (Dušková, 1988:272)

Time reference of postmodifying participial *-ing* forms is that of the finite verb in the main clause as exemplified below:

(26) *The person who will write/writes/wrote reports is my colleague.* (CGEL, 1985:1263)

(27) *The person writing reports is my colleague.* (CGEL, 1985:1263)

Postmodifying participial *-ing* forms "should not be seen as abbreviated progressive forms in relative clauses. Stative verbs, for instance, which cannot have the progressive in the finite verb phrase, can appear in participial form." (CGEL, 1985:1263)

(28) *It was a mixture consisting of oil and vinegar.* (CGEL, 1985: 1263)

(29) *the man who is working / works behind the desk* (CGEL, 1985: 1263)

(30) *the man working behind the desk* (CGEL, 1985: 1264)

As demonstrated above the verbal nature of gerundial and participial *-ing* forms functioning as modifiers within noun phrases is diminished as they do not show the full scale of verbal categories.

4. Structural and syntactic analysis of verbal nouns, gerunds and participles identified in the texts of Law Reports.

The following examples selected from our syntactic analysis of the Law Reports corpus shall demonstrate the syntatctic potential of the surveyed *-ing*-forms.

Subject

Verbal noun

1. It will however require the parties and the court to consider in each case whether the proper working[971VN] of the administration of justice requires there to be continuing[972Part] confidentiality after the end of proceedings[973DN].: 971VN – head of a NP, NP – S (FD)

Gerund

2. "It seems to me to be a far cry from questioning[581G] whether the landlord could reasonably carry out those works which he intended if the absence of possession meant that their being[582G] carried out would be rendered useless.": 582 passive G – head of a SemiCl, SemiCl – S (CHD)

3. ... there is no point (in the court retaining[1298G] control over the use of documents which have not been published or even, for some purposes, over those which have)]: 1298G – head of a SemiCl, SemiCl – PrepComp, PrepP – extraposed S (absolute construction) (CHD)

Subject complement

Verbal noun

4. Finally, by way of overview and before turning[361G] to the detail of this case, I add that an eggshell tenancy such as this is a letting[362VN] of an enclosed space which the tenant will use and occupy as such...: 362VN – head of a NP, NP – C_S (CHD)

Gerund

5. 'Obtaining[541G] possession of the holding[542DN]' (sc by the landlord) must, in my view, mean putting[543G] an end to such rights of possession of the holding[544DN] as are vested in the tenant under the terms of his current tenancy.: 543G – head of a SemiCl, SemiCl – C_S (CHD)

Participle

6. I too recognise that these decisions are binding[571Part]: 571Part – head of a SemiCl – C_S(CHD)

7. How that issue could require six lever arch files of evidence, is baffling[1397Part]: 1397Part – head of a SemiCl, SemiCl – C_S (CHD)

Prepositional subject complement

Verbal noun

8. … since such a construction would amount (to a rewriting[12VN] of the contract by which the parties had agreed to be bound;) …: 12VN – head of a NP, NP – PrepC_S(CHD)

Participle

9. … the question arises what approach the court should adopt to any "contraindications" in a lease which might be read (as suggesting[195Part] the finality of time limits set for steps to be taken in a rent review clause.): 195Part – head of a SemiCl, SemiCl – PrepComp, PrepP – PrepC_S(CHD)

10. … the intention of the House of Lords in determining[224G] that there was a presumption that time was to be treated (as not being[225Part] of the essence in rent review clauses) was to do away with the "unfortunate" dichotomy by providing[226] a clear rule, though one subject to an exception.: 225Part – head of a SemiCl, SemiCl – PrepComp, PrepP – PrepC_S(CHD)

11. … so the parties agree that the tenant is to be treated (as having[232Part] agreed that increased rent.): 232 perfect Part – head of a SemiCl, SemiCl – PrepComp, PrepP – PrepC_S(CHD)

12. I think in the present case that the tile work which lines the wall, the wooden floorboards covered by a metallic surface which constitute the demised floor and the roller shutter which provides the enclosure of the fourth side of the shop are all capable of being[422G] described (as having[423Part] been constructed) or at least meaningfully of being[424G] demolished, …: 423 passive perfect Part – head of a SemiCl, SemiCl – PrepComp, PrepP – PrepC_S(CHD)

Prepositional object complement

Participle

13. He relied on other provisions of the rent review clause, such as a provision enabling[264Part] the tenant to call for a review notice and a provision for the interim payment of the landlord's rent figure in the review notice, (as pointing[265Part] to the conclusion that the parties intended time to be of the

essence.): 265Part – head of a SemiCl, SemiCl – PrepComp, PrepP – $PrepC_O$(CHD)

14. As a matter of fact and degree I think that that point is reached in this case and the tenant is not entitled to rely on section 31A (as precluding[590Part] a finding[591DN] that the landlord could not reasonably carry out the works which I have held are within section 30(1)(f) without obtaining[592G] possession.): 590Part – head of a SemiCl, SemiCl – PrepComp, PrepP – $PrepC_O$(CHD)

Object

Direct object

Verbal noun

15. They involve **the complete stripping[403VN] out of all the products and services within the shop**; ...: 403VN – head of a NP, NP – O_D(CHD)

Gerund

16. Nevertheless any unreasonable delay caused by the landlords and which is to the tenants' prejudice would prevent the rent being[59G] revised after the review date.: 59passiveG – head of a SemiCl, SemiCl – O_D (absolute construction) (CHD)

17. *Mecca Leisure* again involved the court considering[87G] a deeming[88G] provision in a rent review clause.: 87G – head of a SemiCl, SemiCl – O_D (absolute construction) (CHD)

Prepositional object

Verbal noun

18. We believe there is a need for rationalisation of the law and practice relating[1441Part] (to reporting[1442VN] of family proceedings[1443DN]) to remove unnecessary complexity and inconsistency and to establish provisions which are as clear and simple as possible while retaining[1444Part] flexibility where necessary.: 1442VN – head of a NP, NP – PrepComp, PrepP – O_{Prep}(FD)

Gerund

19. Further, in referring[285G] (to the clause being[286G] a trap) he ignores the remarks made by Sir John Donaldson MR in *AWADA* p 615...: 286G – head of a SemiCl, SemiCl – PrepComp, PrepP – O_{Prep} (absolute construction) (CHD)

20. There must, however, in my judgment, come a point where the necessity of permitting[588G] the tenant to undo what the landlord intends would leave so little purpose (in the landlord's doing[589G] what he intends) that he could not

reasonably do that which he otherwise intends without possession.: 589G – head of a SemiCl, SemiCl – PrepComp, PrepP – O_{Prep} (CHD)

21. I shall assume that these views are correct and could lead (to terms being[685G] introduced into the new tenancy that allow such works to be done) ...: 685passiveG – head of a SemiCl, SemiCl – PrepComp, PrepP – O_{Prep} (absolute construction) (CHD)

Gerund – adjective complementation
22. ... he regarded the terms of each of clause 4 and of clause 7 as quite inconsistent (with time not being[300G] of the essence).: 300G – head of a SemiCl, SemiCl – PrepComp, PrepP – O_{Prep} (absolute construction) (CHD)

23. The judge held that the premises, although comprising[320Part] only the internal skin of the part of the building[321DN] occupied by the tenant, were capable (of being[322G] demolished) ...: 322 passive G – head of a SemiCl, SemiCl – PrepComp, PrepP – O_{Prep}(CHD)

Premodifier
Gerund
24. (the deeming[6G] provision): 6G – head of a SemiCl, SemiCl – Premod in a NP

25. (negotiating[287G] purposes): 287G – head of a SemiCl, SemiCl – Premod in a NP (CHD)

26. (17 to 23 working[459G] days): 459G – head of a SemiCl, SemiCl – Premod in a NP (CHD)

27. (a letting[684G] space which incorporates other units on the ground floor): 684G – head of a SemiCl, SemiCl – Premod in a NP (CHD)

28. (an improved filling[724G] station that could be occupied without further work being[725] done): 724G – head of a SemiCl, SemiCl – Premod in a NP (CHD)

Participle
29. (two apparently conflicting[5Part] decisions of the Court of Appeal): 5Part – head of a SemiCl, SemiCl – Premod in a NP (CHD)

30. (the contracting[8Part] parties): 8Part – head of a SemiCl, SemiCl – Premod in a NP (CHD)

31. (the surrounding[89Part] circumstances): 89Part – head of a SemiCl, SemiCl – Premod in a NP (CHD)

Postmodifier

Verbal Noun

32. In *AWADA* the lease contained [provision (for the serving[65VN] of a notice and a counter-notice)] ...: 65VN – head of a NP, NP – PrepComp, PrepP – Postmod in a NP (CHD)

33. ... the principle that provisions for [the service (of the serving[118VN] of notices and counter-notices within specified times)] constitute mere machinery for the ascertainment of the open market rent from time to time requires one to apply the presumption unless the contraindications are clear.: 118VN – head of a NP, NP – PrepComp, PrepP – Postmod in a NP (CHD)

Gerund

34. In Mecca Leisure Ltd v Renown Investments Ltd (1984) 49 P&CR 12. the Court of Appeal held that such a provision did not have [the effect (of rebutting[20G] the presumption that time was not of the essence of a contract)]: 20G – head of a SemiCl, SemiCl – PrepComp, PrepP – Postmod in a NP (CHD)

35. There is [no proper basis (for distinguishing[46G] the facts of this case from *Mecca Leisure*)]: 46G – head of a SemiCl, SemiCl – PrepComp, PrepP – Postmod in a NP (CHD)

36. For these reasons I am of the opinion that [the equitable rule (against treating[61G] time as of the essence of a contract)] is applicable to rent review clauses unless there is some special reason for excluding[62G] its application to a particular clause.: 61G – head of a SemiCl, SemiCl – PrepComp, PrepP – Postmod in a NP (CHD)

37. If, however, one assumes, as one must, that [the doctrine (of time not being[117G] of the essence)] applies to rent review clauses, ...: 117G – head of a SemiCl, SemiCl – PrepComp, PrepP – Postmod in a NP (absolute cosntruction)

38. I would reach the clear conclusion that the parties intended that the time limit specified in paragraph (1) should be strictly observed because of [the consequences (of failing[246G] to do so spelt out in paragraph 2.)]: 246G – head of a SemiCl, SemiCl – PrepComp, PrepP – Postmod in a NP (CHD)

Participle

39. On 30 March 1999 the landlord served (a notice proposing[2Part] a new annual rent of L84,800 with effect from 1 August 1999.): 2Part – head of a SemiCl, SemiCl – Postmod in a NP (CHD)

40. The issue in the case was whether the tenant of the premises could serve a counter-notice in respect of a rent review notice served by the landlord notwithstanding[24Prep] the fact that the time provided for such a counter-notice in the lease had elapsed and the lease contained (a clause deeming[25Part] the rent sought by the landlord to be the new rent if no such counter-notice was served in time.): 25Part – head of a SemiCl, SemiCl – Postmod in a NP (CHD)

41. By a lease dated 21 February 1984, the predecessors in title of the landlord granted to the predecessors in title of the defendant a lease of a piece of land in Boscombe, near Bournemouth, Dorset for (a term of 21 years beginning[28Part] on 1 August 1992,) at an initial rent of L18,000 per annum.: 28Part – head of a SemiCl, SemiCl – Postmod in a NP (CHD)

Adverbial of accompanying circumstances – time

Verbal noun

42. It is not to be seen as an independent clause creating[279Part] a binding[280Part] obligation (on the happening[281VN] of a particular event): 281VN – head of a NP, NP – PrepComp, PrepP – Adv accomp/of time (CHD)

Gerund

43. (Before turning[27G] to consider the law), it is necessary to set out briefly the facts of this case which were not the subject of dispute.: 27G – head of a SemiCl, SemiCl – PrepComp, PrepP – Adv of accomp/time (dangling construction) (CHD)

44. The period of one month provided in the rent review clause elapsed (without any counter-notice being[37G] served.): 37 passive G – head of a SemiCl, SemiCl – PrepComp, PrepP – Adv of accomp/time (absolute construction) (CHD)

45. (In reaching[153G] such a conclusion) I am comforted that that view is entirely consistent with the conclusion of Browne-Wilkinson LJ in *Mecca Leisure, …*: 153G – head of a SemiCl, SemiCl – PrepComp, PrepP – Adv of accomp/time (CHD)

Participle

46. The landlord, Starmark Enterprises Ltd, having[13Part] subsequently acquired the reversionary interest of the leasehold, had its name substituted…: 13 perfect Part – head of a SemiCl, SemiCl – Adv of accomp/time (CHD)

47. Foreseeing[110Part] the problems that have arisen since as a result of the decision of the majority in *Mecca Leisure*, Browne-Wilkinson LJ commented p 24...: 110 Part – head of a SemiCl, SemiCl – Adv of accomp/time (CHD)

48. Therefore, with regret, I cannot agree that the matter depends in each case on the exact detailed drafting[112DN] of the rent review clause, the existence of a provision for a default rent being[113Part] merely one of the factors to be taken into account in deciding[114G] whether time is of the essence.: 113Part – head of a SemiCl, SemiCl – Adv of accomp/time (absolute construction) (CHD)

49. ... the parties intended that time should be of the essence, particularly when dealing[137Part] with the response of a lessee to whom the contract did not give the same leniency in the matter of notice as to the lessor.: 137 Part – head of a SemiCl, SemiCl – Adv of accomp/time (CHD)

Adverbial of contingency – reason:

Verbal noun

50. ... any goodwill which shall have become attached to the demised premises since the commencement of the term hereby granted (by reason of the carrying[178VN] on thereat of the business of the lessees) ...: 178VN – head of a SemiCl, SemiCl – PrepComp, PrepP – Adv of reason (CHD)

Gerund

51. He instituted proceedings[1172DN] to commit her, her solicitor and others for contempt of court (for disclosing[1173G] information about the nullity hearing[1174DN]) ...: 1173G – head of a SemiCl, SemiCl – PrepComp, PrepP – Adv of reason (dangling construction) (CHD)

Participle

52. I agree to the destruction of the subject matter of the original holding[655DN], but I demand that, it having[656Part] been destroyed, I am granted a new tenancy, not of my holding[657DN], but of some entirely different entity.: 656Part – head of a SemiCl, SemiCl – Adv of reason (absolute construction) (CHD)

53. That being[1525Part] the narrow issue I find it difficult to discern a sufficiently clear duty in the court to give rise to a corresponding[1526Part] duty on the parties to refrain from ulterior use of the litigation material.: 1525Part – head of a SemiCl, SemiCl – Adv of reason (absolute construction) (FD)

Adverbial of contingency – purpose:
Gerund
54. Slade LJ added, at p 624: "One cannot invoke the principles of *United Scientific* (for the purpose of rejecting[84G] a provision which clearly indicates the parties' intention that time *is* to be of the essence for the purpose of a rent review clause.)": 84G – head of a SemiCl, SemiCl – PrepComp, PrepP – Adv of purpose (CHD)

55. But the process should not be allowed to place upon the litigant any harsher or more oppressive burden than is strictly required (for the purpose of securing[1291G] that justice is done) ...: 1291G – head of a SemiCl, SemiCl – PrepComp, PrepP – Adv of purpose (dangling construction) (FD)

Adverbial of contingency – result:
Participle
56. There is nothing to prevent parties agreeing[230G] that time should be of the essence, thereby defeating[231Part] the presumption, provided that that agreement is clearly indicated in the lease. 231Part – head of a SemiCl, SemiCl – Adv of result (dangling construction) (CHD)

57. Part IV applications do not necessarily come within section 12 of the 1960 Act nor is the element of compulsion, thereby triggering[1368Part] an implied undertaking[1369DN], always present.: 1368Part – head of a SemiCl, SemiCl – Adv of result (dangling construction) (CHD)

Adverbial of contingency – condition:
Participle
58. In *AWADA* the lease contained provision for the serving[65VN] of a notice and a counter-notice and failing[66Part] agreement as to the market rent, for the appointment of a surveyor.: 66Part – head of SemiCl, SemiCl – Adv of condition (dangling construction) (CHD)

Adverbial of contingency – concession:
Participle
59. Viscount Dilhorne, although agreeing[52Part] with the conclusion in respect of each case, clearly took a different view as to the general proposition.: 52Part – head of a SemiCl, SemiCl – Adv of concession (CHD)

60. Griffiths LJ, while concurring[260Part] in the result, reached the same conclusion by a different route.: 260 Part – head of a SemiCl, SemiCl – Adv of concession (CHD)

Adverbial of process – manner by comparison:
Verbal noun
61. He decided that the confidentiality afforded to disclosure of means made by a party under compulsion in matrimonial proceedings[1323DN] was a matter of great public importance which weighed [more heavily (than the giving[1324VN] of security for costs)] and refused the application.: 1324VN – head of a NP, NP PrepComp, PrepP – degree complement of Adverb, Adverb Phrase – Adv of manner by comparison (FD)

Adverbial of process – means:
Gerund
62. The landlord's surveyors responded (by pointing[41G] out that the counter-notice was served outside the time provided by the rent review clause.): 41G – head of SemiCl, SemiCl – PrepComp, PrepP – Adv of means (CHD)

Apposition
63. Where I differ from the Court of Appeal is upon the crucial question of construction of the words 'without obtaining[536G] possession of the holding[537DN]'.: 536G – head of a SemiCl, SemiCl – Apposition (CHD)

64. However, in my judgment, *Heath v Drown* applies to (i) a consideration of the effect of the relevant terms of (a) the new lease, whether they are introduced therein pursuant section 31A or section 35, and (b) the existing[552Part] tenancy (as continued by section 24 of the 1954 Act); and (ii) the statutory phrase "obtaining[553G] possession of the holding[554DN]" in both section 30(1)(f) and section 31A.: 553G – head of a SemiCl, SemiCl – Apposition (CHD)

CHAPTER THREE

Law Reports under syntactic analysis

This section is aimed to summarise and comment on the findings revealed in the course of surveying the total occurrence of *-ing* forms in the Law Reports corpus and their word-class assignment in order to exemplify the mode of interpreting the findings, following the above syntactic analysis.

Table 1. The total of *-ing* forms occurring in the Law Reports corpus.

Items	Number	Percentage
deverbal noun	627	40.20 %
verbal noun	26	1.60 %
Gerund	397	25.50 %
participle	373	24.00 %
main verb	28	1.80 %
auxiliary	3	0.20 %
infinitive	0	0.00 %
adjective	33	2.10 %
preposition	56	3.60 %
conjunction	1	0.06 %
excluded	14	0.90 %
total of *-ing* forms	1.558	100.00 %
total of words	51.614	–

Table 1. shows the distribution of the total of *-ing* forms as they were assigned to respective word classes. 14 items are ambiguous as to the word-class to be ranked with due to lack of context and are therefore excluded from the total number of the analysed *-ing* forms.

There are 28 cases where an *-ing* form functions as main verb in a complex finite verb phrase, *eg:*

(1) *Alternatively it was submitted that since the court was **construing**[45MainVerb] a different contract from that in Mecca Leisure the court was not bound by that decision.* (CHD)

There are 3 cases of an *-ing* form functioning as auxiliary indicating the progressive aspect in a passive finite verb phrase (see Supplement Two, p. 21), *eg:*

(2) *I too recognise that these decisions are binding[571Part] but in my judgment the difficulties in the interpretation and application of section 31A*

recognised in them have the result that their extent should be examined with care when they are ***being***[572Aux] *considered in a different factual matrix.* (CHD)

There are several cases where the function of the *-ing* forms seems to be ambiguous between indicating the progressive aspect in an infinitive construction and that of the participial premodifier in a noun phrase, the possibility of replacing the verb *to be* by *eg to exist, to remain,* however, justifies the latter interpretation satisfactorily:

(3) *It will however require the parties and the court to consider in each case whether the proper working*[1381VN] *of the administration of justice requires there* ***to be (to remain, to exist) continuing***[1382Part] ***confidentiality*** *after the end of the proceedings*[1383DN]. (FD)

The frequency of the *-ing* forms indicating the progressive aspect in a complex finite verb phrase is, as the table shows, rather low (only in 28 cases, *ie* 1.8 % of the total).

The prepositional status was assigned to 56 occurrences of *-ing* forms, the status of conjunction to 1 *-ing* form, *ie notwithstanding that.* The Compact Oxford English Dictionary recognises the following *-ing* forms as prepositions: *during, pending*; The New Shorter Oxford English Dictionary recognises as prepositions: *during, following, including, notwithstanding, according to* of those *-ing* forms which occur in our texts. These are the cases of functional shift where an *-ing* participle started to function as preposition *ie* head of a prepositional phrase and is complemented by a prepositional complement (noun phrases or gerundial semi-clause constructions). As an example we may submit the form *during.* One of the entries for this form in the Compact Oxford English Dictionary provides the following information at p.486, 1134: "*during* – present participle and preposition. The present participle of *DURE* (verb) = *enduring, lasting, continuing,* was used in French and English in a construction derived from the Latin 'ablative absolute', thus the Latin *vita durante*, Old French *vie durant*, English *life during* = *while life endured or endures*. The participle also often stood before the substantive, *eg* Latin *durante bello*, French *durant la guerre*, English *during the war,* in which construction *during* came in modern language to be treated as preposition: *throughout the whole continuance of,* hence *in the course of, in the time of.*"

Similarly, Jespersen holds that: "A complete transition to being a preposition from this construction (*ie* construction where the first participle precedes the subject) has taken place with *during, pending.* … The complete transition is seen in the possibility of saying: *during and after the crisis. Notwithstanding* is used in a corresponding way, either before or after its subject...; if followed by a clause it may now be considered a conjunction." (Jespersen, 1965e:51)

Jespersen points to the fact that the prepositional status of some of the *-ing* forms may have evolved from their occurrence in the constructions known as 'loose participles' (*ie dangling participles*):

(4) *Considering his age, your conduct is scandalous.* (Jespersen, 1965e: 410)

(5) *One may bivouack decently, barring rain and wind, up to the end of October.* (Jespersen, 1965e: 410)

(6) *There may be nothing new under and including the sun.* (Jespersen, 1965e:410)

Proceeding further to the issue of *-ing* forms functioning as adjectives, we identified the following examples of *-ing* forms:

- in **attributive function**:
  A) *the deeming provision, negotiating purposes, working days, a letting space, an improved filling station, refitting works, a dwelling house, the housing needs and resources, the balancing exercise, reporting restrictions, the starting point;*
  B) *two apparently conflicting decisions, the contracting parties, the following judgments, the surrounding circumstances, the two competing arguments, the dissenting judgment, the corresponding provision, an agreed and binding obligation, the foregoing provisions, the existing design, the underlying brickwork, the adjoining shop, the dividing wall, the contrasting decisions, a subsisting tenancy, less compelling points, enclosing walls, occupying tenants of business premises, the guiding principle, the underlying principle, the changing forensic practice, damaging disclosures, ringing tones, an enduring problem, the rolling programme, the increasing influence, sweeping reforms, those conflicting considerations;*
  C) *the ongoing problems, a willing lessor, (non-) load-bearing parts of the building, the overriding principle, this far-reaching physical effect, the most interesting submissions, the surprising absence of authority, any pending proceedings;*
- and in **predicative function**
  it would be surprising, if it is willing, which are not load-bearing, it might be thought to be inconvenient and time-consuming, the provisions are not binding, it is baffling.

The criteria for identifying *-ing* forms as adjectives include *inter alia* the possibility of gradation, intensification by *very*, basis for word-formation processes, admissibility of alteration of a copular verb. The *-ing* forms in the predicative function may be subject to the alteration of a copular verb test which aids in singling out the *-ing* forms functioning as *-ing* subject complement from those which operate as main verbs of complex finite verb phrases indicating the progressive aspect. We may then apply the rest of the criteria to the *-ing* forms which function as subject complements and attributes. At this point, it will have to be noticed, however, that the testing may not provide satisfactory outcome as to the definite word class assignment. See example 1397 below:

(7) *How that issue could require six lever arch files of evidence, is baffling*[1397]. (FD)

First we apply the admissibility of alteration of a copular verb test (*ie it seems baffling*) and we find that this *-ing* form does not function as the main verb in a complex finite verb phrase. Now we should apply the rest of the criteria: *it is very baffling, even more baffling, bafflingly*. It seems to satisfy all the criteria for the full-fledged adjective status, still, the New Shorter Oxford Dictionary does not assign it to the word class of adjectives. On the other hand, not all of the *-ing* forms recognised by the dictionaries as adjectives possess all of these features, and are, nevertheless, identified as adjectives by the above mentioned dictionary, *eg pending* (**very/more pending, *pendingly*).

The test of admissibility of a copular verb other than to be is also applicable, as mentioned before, as a means of distinguishing the *-ing* form functioning as head of the infinitive in the progressive from that of a participial premodifier in a noun phrase, see the sentence (8) below:

(8) *Goulding J said, at pp 713 – 714, that the principle of the implied undertaking*[1318DN] *"rests on a wider ground, namely, that public interest requires that a party, compelled by process of law to make what* ***may be (seem) damaging***[1319Part] ***disclosures*** *for the purpose of a particular suit, should not thereby be at risk of their use for other purposes. It is a strong thing, though necessary for matrimonial litigation, to make a man disclose all the details of his means."* (FD)

The example (8) may also serve to demonstrate that a mistaken interpretation (head of the infinitive in the progressive *vs* participial premodifier) may result in a different semantic interpretation of the sentence, *ie*:

a) to take steps that may damage disclosures for the purpose of a particular suit – for the progressive infinitive;
b) to make disclosures that may be damaging in effect – for the participial premodifier.

Here the latter interpretation is definitely supported by the sentential context.

Thus if we do not intend the dividing line between the *-ing* adjectives and *-ing* participles as premodifiers or subject complements to seem rather arbitrary, we must admit that the sharp dividing line does not actually exist and we should rather speak of the process of transition taking place, enabling the *-ing* forms in the function of premodifier and subject complement to be approached in terms of scale whose one end would be occupied by the central adjectives *eg surprising, interesting*, the other end by the participial adjectives performing this function *ad hoc* (this feature being a rather productive source of the *-ing* premodifier occurrences) *eg subsisting, occupying, damaging,* with more or less adjectivally established *-ing* forms placed between these two ends *eg existing, competing, surrounding pending, outstanding, baffling*. This conclusion is also supported by the fact that the consulted dictionaries do not always concur in the assignment of the respective *-ing* forms in these syntactic functions to the word class of adjectives or participial adjectives or simply verb forms.

For the purposes of the present analysis, however, we have had to determine the assignment and we therefore refer to the New Shorter Oxford English Dictionary which recognises the following *-ing* forms as full-fledged adjectives: *overriding, interesting, pending, time-consuming, ongoing, surprising, willing, load-bearing*. The rest of the *-ing* premodifiers and subject complements is ranked with either gerunds – group A above or participles – group B above.

The rest of the *-ing* forms, occurring in our corpus, were ranked with either deverbal nouns, *-ing* verbal nouns, gerunds or participles.

627 items were assigned the status of deverbal nouns on account of their semantics and morpho-syntactic potential identified in the particular context: *building, beginning, ceiling, claddings, covering, drafting, drawings, earnings, feeling, finding, fittings, footing, heading, hearing, holding, meaning, misunderstanding, plastering, proceedings, reasoning, pleadings, sub-heading, tiling, understanding, undertaking, upbringing, warning, well-being, wiring, wording.*

Semantic criterion (*ie* conveyance of processuality as secondary predication) along with purely nominal indicators in a particular syntactic context led us in extracting *-ing* verbal nouns. We must admit, however, that in some cases it is rather difficult to decide whether an *-ing* form functions as deverbal noun or verbal noun due to that fact that the *-ing* ending, (as pointed out in Chapter One herein, p. 30), is capable of functioning as gap-filler for the category of deverbal nouns and non-*ing* verbal nouns.

From the semantic point of view, we may therefore make a choice between one of the three options for *eg* the word *hearing* occurring in our texts:

deverbal noun interpretation (*ie* event of hearing a case), non-*ing* verbal noun interpretation (*ie* action of hearing a case as abstract concept) and *-ing*-verbal noun interpretation (*ie* action of hearing a case conceived processually). We may demonstrate it by the following set of sentences comprising the word *hearing*.

(9) *There is no statutory prohibition against providing*[1236G] *for* ***hearings***[1237DN] *in chambers in the family cases;* (FD)

(10) *Those proceedings*[1040DN] *were adjourned pending*[1041Prep] *the* ***hearing***[1042DN] *before Munby J and on appeal.* (FD)

(11) *The* ***hearing***[1222DN] *or consideration shall, unless the court otherwise directs, take place in chambers.* (FD)

(12) *Among the directions for the* ***hearing***[1170DN] *of the petition was that the cause be heard in camera.* (FD)

(13) *Unless the court otherwise directs, a* ***hearing***[1226DN] *of, or directions appointment in,* ***proceedings***[1227DN] *to which this Part applies shall be in chambers.* (FD)

(14) *The* ***hearing***[1206DN] *of cases is divided into those which are heard in open court and those heard in chambers.* (FD)

The above examples are more or less ambiguous between the concrete 'event' interpretation and that of 'abstract action' interpretation. The former is perhaps more plausible in the first three examples, while the latter seems to be more suitable in respect of the sentences (12), (13) and (14). As in the present research non-*ing* verbal nouns are excluded from the syntactic analysis, we decided to label all the above *-ing* forms as deverbal nouns, being aware that the issue is ambiguous.

As suggested above, we noticed two shades of meaning: (action viewed as process *vs* abstract concept/fact/single completed act) detectable in respect of the verbal noun existing in two variants, *ie -ing* verbal nouns and verbal nouns formed by suffixes other than *-ing*. Example (15) below may serve: 1) to demonstrate that there are two distinct items existing side by side, and 2) to show the semantic distinctions conveyed by the respective variants:

(15) *If, however, one assumes, as one must, that the doctrine of time not being*[117G] *of the essence applies to rent review clauses, the principle that provisions for the* ***service*** *of the* ***serving***[118VN] *of notices and counter-notices within specified times constitute mere machinery for the ascertainment of*

the open market rent from time to time requires one to apply the presumption unless the contraindications are clear. (CHD)

It may be clear form the above example that the verbal noun *service* is more abstract with general implications as to the rules applicable to the issue of serving notices while the *-ing* verbal noun *serving* is more concrete conveying the process of the action itself in its particular manifestations. This only supports our assumption that the respective types of *-ing* forms (and here also the related category of verbal nouns formed by suffixes other than *-ing*) are not completely identical, but have their structural and semantic specifics which influence the choice of a particular type.

Another aspect demonstrating the separate existence of the above categories of verbal nouns seems to be the fact that only the *-ing* verbal nouns preserve verbal government when postmodified by a noun phrase, *eg the charge of theft vs the charging with theft.*

As the next step we attempted to distinguish between the *-ing* verbal nouns and gerunds, employing the tests outlined in Supplement Two, p. 2. In the absence of the morpho-syntactic indicators (*ie* admissibility/inadmissibility of determination by articles, adjective/adverbial modification, *of*-phrase postmodification/object complementation, distinct morphological forms of the gerund), the only way to distinguish them was to resort to the semantic factor. What seems to be the crucial difference is the factitiveness absent in the semantics of the *-ing* verbal noun. This type is associated primarily with the idea of processuality (it, therefore, cannot be formed from stative verbs.)

Sometimes it is possible to identify the proper status of an *-ing* form by analogy with another *-ing* form, as may be demonstrated by examples occurring in sentences (16) and (17) below which were found in the Acts of Parliament corpus:

(16) ... ***any offence at common law of*** *larceny, robbery, burglary,* ***receiving stolen property****, obtaining property by threats, extortion by colour of office or franchise, false accounting by public officers, concealment of treasure trove and, except as regards offences relating to the public revenue, cheating;* ... (TA)

(17) ... *references in any enactment passed before this Act to an offence abolished by this Act shall, subject to any express amendment or repeal made by this Act, have effect as references to the corresponding offence*

under this Act, and in any such enactment the expression "receive" (when it relates to ***an offence of receiving****) shall mean handle, ...* (TA)

We must, however, point to the fact that in the above examples as well as those in the sentence (18) below the whole constructions are used to denote (various types of offences) rather than to predicate. This common quality enables their simple co-ordination despite the lack of structural uniformity. You may find the four types, which are under review in this section, in the following provision of section 32 (1), Theft Act 1968:

(18) *... any offence at common law of* ***larceny***^{DN}, ***robbery***^{DN}, ***burglary***^{DN}, ***receiving***^{G} ***stolen property, obtaining***^{G} ***property by threats, extortion***$^{non\text{-}ingVN}$ ***by colour of office or franchise, false accounting***$^{-ingVN}$ ***by public officers, concealment***$^{non\text{-}ingVN}$ ***of treasure trove, abstracting***$^{-ingVN}$ ***of electricity;*** (TA)

-Ing verbal nouns and gerunds are often treated as interchangeable variants of one type. Considerations presented in the first chapter of this thesis as well as in Supplement Two may have justified their separate treatment in our research. We will summarise the conditioning factors that may influence the choice of a particular type. First, we will supply some of the observations relevant to the present issue found in Marková (1986:86):

- the use of either variant may change the functional perspective of a sentence, *eg*:

(19) *For Chomsky, a chief task of linguistic theory is to model the functioning of that equipment/that equipment functioning.* (Marková,1986:86)

- inadmissibility of the inflectional genitive with inanimate or abstract nouns, *eg*:

(20) *He welcomed, at least at first the vigour of the cold and even the blowing of the wind.* (Marková,1986:86)

- the use of the article may be motivated:
  - some contexts require a means of expressing the category of definiteness for semantic reasons, *eg*:

(21) *Through a recorded history man has listened and, frequently, has attempted to formalize the listening into one form of religion or another.* (Marková, 1986: 87)

- occurrence of an *-ing* form in a coordinative construction together with a noun (examples (20), (22)). In the latter the stative or resultative conception rather than the procedural one is being indicated by the use of indefinite article, *eg*:

(22) *Even in Wodehouse he felt a hollowness, a turning away from reality that was implicitly bitter and became explicit in the comic figures of futile clergymen.* (Marková,1986:88)

What may be objected to in respect of the tendencies listed above is the fact that except for the *-ing* form in sentence (20), the *-ing* forms, as we assume, may be assigned the status of non-*ing* verbal nouns, *ie* abstract conceptualisations of verbal idea, and therefore cannot be actually taken as relating to the distinction between processual *-ing* verbal nouns and gerunds.

In our opinion, the main conditioning factor in respect of the *-ing* verbal noun/gerund dichotomy is the tendency to use the gerund when it is desirable to evoke the idea of concreteness, factitiveness and inherent implication of the agent. Several examples from the Acts of Parliament corpus may serve to demonstrate the point.

Adverbial of time

(23) *Where an order is made under subsection (1) above in favour of a party to the marriage* ***on or after the granting of a decree of nullity of marriage****, neither the order nor any settlement made in pursuance of the order takes effect unless the decree has been made absolute.* (FLA)

(24) ***On or after granting a decree of nullity of marriage*** *(whether before or after the decree is made absolute), the court may, on application made under this section, make one or more property adjustment orders in relation to the marriage.* (FLA)

Adverbial of means

(25) *The powers of the court under this section to make one or more financial provision orders are exercisable against each party to the marriage* ***by the making of a combined order on one occasion.*** (FLA)

(26) *The court shall exercise its powers under this section, so far as is practicable,* ***by making on one occasion all such provision as can be made by way of one or more property adjustment orders in relation to the marriage*** *as it thinks fit.* (FLA)

Postmodifier

(27) *Where,* ***at a time before the making of a divorce order*** *_an order ("a paragraph (a) order") for the payment of a lump sum has been made under section 22A above in favour of a party, the court may, on an application made jointly by the parties to the marriage, vary or discharge the order.* (FLA)

(28) *In such a case, the court may, on or at* ***any time after making the main order****, make an order ("the order for interest") for the amount deferred, or the installments, to carry interest (at such rate as may be specified in the order for interest) –* (FLA)

Time adverbial in a semi-clause construction

(29) *An order under this section for the payment of a lump sum to or for the benefit of a child of the family may be made for the purpose of enabling any liabilities or expenses reasonably incurred by or for the benefit of that child* ***before the making of an application for an order under this section in his favour*** *to be met.* (FLA)

(30) *An order under this section that a party to a marriage must pay a lump sum to the other party may be made for the purpose of enabling that other party to meet any liabilities or expenses reasonably incurred by him or her in maintaining himself or herself or any child of the family* ***before making an application for an order under this section in his or her favour.*** (FLA)

Adverbial of purpose

(31) *A case also falls within this section* ***for the purposes of the making of a section 1(1)(a) order*** *if that order is made in or in connection with any proceedings for the nullity of the marriage of the parents of the child concerned.* (FLA)

(32) *If, at a full hearing, the court makes an occupation order, then a)* ***for the purposes of calculating the maximum period for which the full order may be made to have effect,*** *the relevant section is to apply as if the period for which the full order will have effect began on the date on which the initial order first had effect;* (FLA)

The *-ing* forms in the above couples of sentences, derived from the same bases with the exception of examples (31) and (32), performing the same syntactic functions, occurring in almost identical semantic settings and implying the same agent (except for the last couple) take the form of gerund where it is necessary to imply active participation of the agent present explicitly in the matrix clause while they have the form of verbal noun where the agent in the matrix clause is absent. The sentence comprising the latter form is thus more impersonal and conceptualised. This seems to be quite consistent with the general tendency concerning the *-ing* verbal noun/gerund dichotomy consisting in the fact that the original verbal valency potential is stronger with the gerund and less intense with the *-ing* verbal noun.

Another tendency that we have noticed concerns the line gerund – verbal noun formed by the suffixes other than *-ing*. The non-*ing* verbal noun seems to be preferred where it is desirable to stress the conceptualisation of the given action without the necessity to express explicitly its agent and to avoid passivisation otherwise required to comply with the attachment rule if the action were to be conveyed by the gerundial *-ing* form, *eg*:

(33) *If after... the **grant**[VN] **of/being granted**[G] a decree annulling a marriage either spouse remarries, that spouse is not entitled to apply, by reference to the making of that order or the grant of that decree, for Part II order.* (FLA)

(34) *... that a party, compelled by process of law to make what may be damaging*[1319Part] *disclosures for the purpose of a particular suit, should not thereby be at risk of **their use**[VN]**/their being used**[G] for other purpose.* (FD)

(35) *They involve the removal of the roller shutter which forms the shop's frontage and **its replacement**[VN]**/its being replaced**[G] by a show window extending*[408Part] *in front of all shops with the entrance into no 13.* (CHD)

(36) *Privately, the liberals admitted that the Humphrey amendment had no chance of **passage**[VN]**/being passed**[G].* (the Brown Corpus 1979)

Stylistic motives should not be omitted either, as the combination of different structural variants seems preferable to cumulation of variants of the same kind, with the gerundial action being definitely more processual than that of the verbal noun from the semantic point of view, *eg*:

(37) *Subsection (4) – (b) does not apply if the court is satisfied that **delaying the making of a divorce order/*making a divorce order** would be significantly detrimental to the welfare of any child of the family;* (FLA)

(38) *The circumstances referred to in section 9(7)(b) are that... d) **a delay/*delaying in making the order applied for under section 3-** (i) would be significantly detrimental to the welfare of any child of the family;* (FLA)

On the other hand, in co-ordinative constructions, the variants of the same structural type are desirable, *eg*:

(39) *They involve the complete* ***stripping***[403VN] *out of all the products and services within the shop; the* ***cutting***[404VN] *back of the surfaces of the walls which contain the shop to the underlying*[405Part] *brickwork and, in the case of the wall between numbers 9 and 11 (the adjoining*[406Part] *shop) the* ***removal***[VN] *of 60 to 70 % of the wall;* ***replacing***[407G] *the support that wall gives to the upper floors by a steel column to be positioned outside the area of the demise; the* ***removal***[VN] *of the roller shutter which forms the shop's frontage and its replacement by a show window extending*[408Part] *in front of all four shops with the entrance into no 13;* (CHD)

where examples 403 and 404 are structurally equivalent to the verbal noun **removal** and ex 407gerund seems to disturb the stylistic demand for the structural uniformity of coordinated items. Nevertheless, such deviation is not unusual, *eg*:

(40) *To hold that time was not of the essence of the tenant's counter-notice would involve not simply* ***extending***[127G] *the time limits within which the parties' bargain could be formed but an* ***alteration***[VN] *of the parties' bargain itself.* (CHD)

Another sort of motivation for the mixture of different structural forms may be detected in the second sentence of example (41) where the co-ordinative construction consisting of gerundial semi-clause components is interrupted by a noun phrase headed by a verbal noun in order to avoid inappropriate classification of the *-ing* form *following* as preposition:

(41) *The European Economic Community was created by the Treaty of Rome with the broad object of furthering economic development within the Community by the establishment of a Common Market and the approximation of the economic policies by the member states. Its more detailed aims included* ***eliminating*** *customs duties internally and* ***adopting*** *a common customs tariff externally,* ***the following by member states of common policies on agriculture and transport, promoting*** *the free movement of labour and capital between member states, and* ***outlawing*** *within the community all practices leading to the distortion of competition.* (Dictionary of Law, 2006, p. 202).

The necessity to avoid inappropriate syntactic classification of an *-ing* form ambiguous between the gerund and verbal noun may also be demonstrated by the following examples:

(42) *material for the wrapping of paper versus*

(43) *material for wrapping paper.*

The *-ing* form in (42) functions as head of a noun phrase complementing the preposition *for* with the prepositional phrase postmodifying the head *material*. The *-ing* form in (43) must be taken as premodifier of the head *paper*. The importance of distinguishing between the respective potential syntactic interpretations of the constructions is justified by the resulting semantic differences: the meaning of (42) is 'material necessary for the activity of wrapping', while the meaning of (43) is 'material for the production of wrapping paper'.

In ex (44) below, the verbal noun choice is necessitated by the use of the referential adverbials *thereof/hereof* employed to avoid repetition of items. These can be used only with the verbal noun as the gerund takes direct object, *eg*:

(44) *This includes, inter alia, purchasing of stock and other securities and disposing thereof.* (private instrument)

The ratio of occurrences of verbal nouns (6.2 %) to gerunds (93.8 %) is approximately 1:15. This is 2.5-times higher in favour of the gerund than the one that was detected in the texts of Acts of Parliament where the ratio was 1:6 in favour of the gerund in the total of 528 items of verbal nouns and gerunds. If we compare this ratio with that stated by Marková (1986:85), *ie* 1:20, we may assume that the impersonal style of the language of the statutory law may account for the higher ratio of verbal noun occurrences whereas the wording of judgments seems to be more flexible as to the possibility of using the variants which are more processual and factitive (*ie* gerunds). These corpus data should support the assertion that the stylistic factor may be included among the rest of the conditioning factors, stated above, which influence the choice between the -*ing* verbal noun and gerund.

The last step in the first stage of our analysis consisted in separating the gerundial semi-clause constructions from the participial ones in the syntactic functions shared by both the types: adverbial, postmodification and premodification. As for the adverbial syntactic function, the basic criterion for the gerundial assignment was 1) the complementation of preposition and 2) the possibility of potential insertion of an agent in the possessive case.

We identified 397 cases of gerunds (51.5 %) and 373 cases of participles (48.5 %). As can be seen, the ratio of occurrences of gerunds to participles is approximately 1:1, gerunds slightly outnumbering participles. In the course of analysis we faced several issues that had to be settled in order to arrive at a uniform structural and syntactic classification.

One of them concerned semi-clause constructions headed by the *-ing* forms complementing prepositions in the adverbial syntactic function. The following examples may serve to demonstrate the point:

(45) *... the landlord could not reasonably carry out the intended work (without obtaining[324G] possession of the premises)* ... (CHD)

(46) *The period of one month provided in the rent review clause elapsed (without any counter notice being[37G] served.)* (CHD)

By reference to the above criteria for distinguishing between gerunds and participles in the adverbial syntactic function, we arrived at the following conclusion as to the structural interpretation of the above types of semi-clauses: the semi-clause constructions in both sentences were classed as gerunds on account of:

a) the fact that they complement a preposition (although it may be argued that the status of the prepositions *without* and *with* is close to that of the conjunctions), and
b) a potential possibility to insert the agent of the secondary predication in the possessive case, *eg*:

(47) *... to obtain possession the landlord has to terminate the current tenancy (without it being[547G] followed by a new tenancy.):* 547 passive G – head of a SemiCl, SemiCl – PrepComp, PrepP – Adv of accomp/time (absolute construction) (CHD)

(48) *... I am inclined to think that work such as installation of the shop front might be carried out and then replaced (without its being[583G] unreasonable to carry out the work in the first place.):* 583G – head of a SemiCl, SemiCl – PrepComp, PrepP – Adv of accomp/time (CHD)

Another syntactic issue related to the patterns where the *-ing* complements a preposition concerned the "complex prepositions of the prepositional phrase type or PP prepositions" (Klégr, 1997:51). Complex prepositions are a rather frequent phenomenon in legal English as pointed out by Quirk *et al.*: "Legal English is notable for complex prepositions, the following being among those found mainly in legalistic or bureaucratic usage: *in case of, in default of, in lieu* *of, on pain of, in respect of.*" (CGEL, 1972:304) We attempted to settle this issue in the course of the preceding stage of our research so we will only briefly repeat the main point. The problem concerns the possibility of dual interpretation of prepositional sequences as either PP prepositions or free sequences of preposition1 + noun phrase + preposition2, depending on the acceptability of a particular item as PP preposition.

The criteria for the prepositional status of an item include replaceability with a lexicalised primary or secondary prepositions, inability to function as an independent clause element (the question test), the invariability of the whole structure in respect of preposition 1 and 2, determiners, and singular or plural form of prep1 complement, irreplaceability of prep1 complement by a semantically related noun and inadmissibility of its premodification, irreplaceability of prep2 complement by the possessive or demonstrative pronoun or impossibility of its complete omission. The criteria were cited in (Klégr, 1997:52 – 53). The spectre of these items forms a graded scale as there is a low percentage of PP prepositions which allow for the variability of prep1, prep2, determiner and singular/plural form of prep1 complement, the distinction between the PP prepositions and free combinations being the matter of degree. "At one extreme, many complex prepositions have close parallels in form and/or meaning with simple prepositions. At the other extreme, four-word free combinations allow considerable variability and are transparent in their meaning. As variability is a matter of degree, it is impossible to establish a clear borderline between free combinations and complex prepositions." (Biber *et al.*, 1999:75 – 76)

Now, we will attempt to show how the assignment of a particular status to a prepositional sequence may influence the syntactic interpretation of its complementing elements (which, in our case, happen to be gerundial semi-clause constructions), *eg*:

(49) *... they have done more than merely mention a timetable* ***for the purpose of ensuring***[218G] ***an orderly review of rent.*** (CHD)

Should we interpret the sequence *for the purpose of* as a well-established PP preposition, the syntactic interpretation of its *-ing* complementation would be that of purpose adverbial. On the other hand, if we take the same sequence as a free combination the resulting syntactic interpretation of the *-ing* form would be: postmodification. In both cases the *-ing* form would be assigned a gerundial status for it complements a preposition.

In the analysed corpus (both Acts of Parliament and Law Reports), we treated the following sequences, complemented by the *-ing* forms, as satisfying the above criteria of prepositionalisation. We supply them in semantic types presented in Klégr (1997:64-78):

cause – reason: *in consequence of, by reason of, by virtue of;*
means: *by reference to;*
purpose: *for the/0 purpose/s of, , with a view to, with the intention of;*
respect: *in relation to, with reference to, with respect to.*

As indicated above, the sequence *for the purpose of* seems to be least established as a PP preposition on account of the variability in respect of the occurrence or omission of *the* determiner, the singular/plural form of the prep1 complement, and also omission of prep2 and modification of prep1 complement which can be exemplified as follows:

(50) *The terms of the new tenancy referred to in section 31A(1)(a) are [**for the limited purpose (of** giving[629G] the landlord access and other facilities to carry out the work it intends to do)], and the Decca case makes clear that what the court has to consider is those works.: 629G – head of a SemiCl, SemiCl – PrepComp, PrepP – Postmod in a NP* (CHD)

(51) ***(For the purposes of** deciding[785G] this appeal) it does not matter which.: 785G – head of a SemiCl, SemiCl – PrepComp, PrepP – Adv of purpose (dangling construction* (CHD)*)*

(52) *Goulding J said, at pp 713 – 714, that the principle of the implied undertaking[1318DN] "rests on a wider ground, namely, that public interest requires that a party, compelled by process of law to make what may be damaging[1319Part] disclosures **for the purpose of** a particular suit, should not thereby be at risk of their use **for other purposes**."* (FD)

The syntactic interpretation of the PP preposition complemented by a gerund (this also concerns the complementation of simple prepositions) depends also on the word-class status of the word which is being complemented. In the following example, the sequence PP + gerund obviously performs the postmodifying syntactic function rather than that of the purpose adverbial (as the case would be if the whole prepositional sequence followed the verb *to enter*):

(53) *... a new tenancy incorporating[532Part] similar terms as respects the landlord's right of [entry (for the purpose of reconstructing[533G] the premises)] as were contained in the current lease.: 533G – head of a SemiCl, SemiCl – PrepComp, PrepP – Postmod in a NP* (CHD)

Another issue concerning the syntactic interpretation consisted in the choice between the gerundial direct or prepositional object whose subject is attached absolutely and participial postmodification of the head of a noun phrase, *eg*:

(54) *Mecca Leisure again involved* ***the court considering***[87] ***a deeming***[88G] ***provision in a rent review clause.*** (CHD)

(55) *It would involve* ***the landlord having***[235] ***to serve a notice…*** (CHD)

(56) *Further, in referring*[285G] *to* ***the clause being***[286] ***a trap*** *he ignores the remarks made by Sir John Donaldson MR in AWADA…* (CHD)

(57) *… a court would agree to* ***a term being***[695] ***included in the new lease that enabled the tenant, or compelled the landlord , to install a floor at the existing***[696Part] ***level.*** (CHD)

The criteria for the gerundial status to be employed here include:

a) the potential replaceability of the subject of the gerundial action in the common case by its possessive counterpart, *ie*:

(58) *Were it otherwise it would involve a tenant's being*[654G] *able to say: '… some entirely different entity.'*: 654G – head of a SemiCl, SemiCl – O_D (absolute construction) (CHD)

b) the possibility to paraphrase the structure by 'the fact that…' rather that by a relative clause 'that which…', *ie* for example sentence (55) it may be paraphrased: *It would involve the fact that the landlord has to serve a notice…* (rather than *It would involve the landlord who has to serve a notice…*, which is normally the participial status indicator)

c) the potential of expressing aspectual contrasts, which is excluded when an *-ing* form functions as postmodifier (see Supplement Two, p. 52) *ie*:

(59) *Section 12 (1) also refers (to the court having*[1104G] *prohibited publication.): 1104perfect G – head of a SemiCl, SemiCl – PrepComp, PrepP –* O_{Prep} *(absolute construction)* (FD)

Thus the semi-clause constructions headed by the *-ing* forms 87, 235, 286, 695 were classified as gerundial with the subject in the common case attached absolutely and the whole structure functioning as direct object in (54) and (55) and prepositional object in (56) and (57).

Jespersen supplies a useful example to support our position that the *-ing* forms exemplified in (54), (55), (56) and (57) form one semantic, structural and syntactic unit: "When Thackeray writes: *'I have not the least objection to a rogue being hung,'* it is not the rogue (who is being hung) that he approves, but his execution – or, grammatically speaking, the object of *to* is not the substantive *rogue,* but the whole combination. … Similarly this analysis is evident in *I hate people being unhappy* (different from 'I hate unhappy people')." (Jespersen, 1966:327).

In respect of the syntactic function of postmodification a similar distinction had to be kept in mind, namely absolute gerundial postmodification *versus* simple participial postmodification of a noun phrase, with the issue being resolved in favour of the former after employing the above-mentioned test, *eg*:

(60) *This dichotomy created [a danger (of distinctions being*[223G] *drawn on narrow and somewhat artificial grounds)].: 223 passive G – head of a SemiCl, SemiCl – PrepComp, PrepP – Postmod in a NP (absolute construction)* (CHD)

(61) *In the final provision there is [a reference (to rent being*[181G] *either actual or deemed)].: 181G – head of a SemiCl, SemiCl – PrepComp, PrepP – Postmod in a NP (absolute construction)* (CHD)

Next, in the syntactic function of gerundial object there occurred two variant structures after the verb *prevent*, one prepositional (62) and one without the preposition *from* (63), the former being ranked with the prepositional object class whereas the latter falling under the syntactic function of direct object in accordance with the above-mentioned criteria that distinguish it from the participial postmodifier:

(62) *There is nothing to prevent the parties (from contracting*[86G] *on this basis) ....:86G – head of a SemiCl, SemiCl – PrepComp, PrepP –* O_{Prep} (CHD)

(63) *There is nothing to prevent parties agreeing*[230G] *that time should be of the essence.: 230G – head of a SemiCl, SemiCl –* O_D *(absolute construction)* (CHD)

Both structures are, in our opinion, rather similar, the variant without the preposition seems to be more condense than the prepositional one.

For the next point let us consider sentences (61), (56) and (59) again.

(61) *In the final provision there is [a* ***reference*** *(to rent being*[181G] *either actual or deemed)].: 181G – head of a SemiCl, SemiCl – PrepComp, PrepP – Postmod in a NP (absolute construction)* (CHD)

(56) *Further, in* ***referring***[285G] *(to the clause being*[286G] *a trap) he ignores the remarks made by Sir John Donaldson MR in AWADA...: 286G – head of a SemiCl, SemiCl – PrepComp, PrepP –* O_{Prep} *(absolute construction)* (CHD)

(59) *Section 12 (1) also* ***refers*** *(to the court having*[1104G] *prohibited publication.): 1104perfect G – head of a SemiCl, SemiCl – PrepComp, PrepP –* O_{Prep} *(absolute construction)* (FD)

We should like to point, once again, to the fact that the interpretation of the syntactic function of a particular construction comprising an *-ing* form depends also on the structural status or word: the class of the word which it complements or modifies. In (61) the word *reference* is a non-*ing* verbal noun, thus the 181 *-ing* form with its common case subject *rent* functions as postmodifier whereas the 1104 *-ing* form in (59) with its subject attached absolutely performs the function of prepositional object of the verb *to refer to*. The fact that we identified the 286 *-ing* form complementing the 285 gerund *referring to* in (56) as prepositional object rather than postmodification seems to be justified by the prevailing verbal character of the gerund preceding it if compared with that of the verbal noun preceding the *-ing* form in sentence (61).

Within the category of gerund we had to make distinction between two types of patterns where the gerund complements the preposition *in*. These may be exemplified by the following corpus instances:

(64) ***The landlord succeeded*** *before the judge* ***in establishing***[820G] *elements (A)(i) and (B).* (FD)

(65) *The grounds of the appeal were that* ***the judge had erred... in failing***[989G] *to give effect to the respondent's rights under articles 6, 8, and 14 of the European Convention for the Protection of Human Rights and Fundamental Freedoms.* (FD)

(66) *The lessee shall indemnify the lessor against the reasonable additional costs* ***incurred*** *by the lessor* ***in carrying***[596G] ***out*** *the intended works.* (CHD)

(67) ***It shall be the duty*** *of the court* ***in deciding***[1483G] *whether to exercise its powers under any of sections 22A to 24BB above and, if so, in what manner, to have regard to all the circumstances of the case...* (FD)

The common feature of these patterns is the fact that the *-ing* item complements the preposition *in* and the whole gerundial construction is related to the verb in the matrix clause. The preposition *in* is, however, capable of introducing both the object of the clause and also time/accompanying circumstances adverbial whose syntactic patterns are similar only seemingly. They are, in fact, distinct on account of a different degree of ties obtaining between the prepositional constructions and the verb to which they are related. These ties are much stronger with the first two examples, *ie* when the function is that of object. In the last two examples the gerundial semi-clauses introduced by *in* are less closely tied to the verb in the matrix clause. The tests that may be employed to distinguish these seemingly quite similar surface structures include contrastive replaceability of the preposition, reduceability of the prepositional phrase to a single word adverb and elicitation by an adverbial question, all indicating the adverbial status (Allerton, 1982:89). This list is extended by Rudanko (1996:9-15) to include admissibility of pseudocleft sentences with the adverbial in the focus position and inadmissibility of right dislocation constructions when the interpretation is intended to be adverbial.

The testing may be exemplified as follows:

- contrastive replaceability of the preposition:

(64) *The landlord succeeded before the judge in/**while*** *establishing*[820G] *elements (A)(i) and (B).* (FD)

(67) *It shall be the duty of the court in/**while** deciding*[1483G] *whether to exercise its powers under any of sections 22A to 24BB above and, if so, in what manner, to have regard to all the circumstances of the case...* (FD)

- reduceability of the prepositional phrase to a single word adverb:

(64) *The landlord succeeded before the judge in **that**.*

(67) *It shall be the duty of the court **then** to have regard to all the circumstances of the case...*

- elicitation by an adverbial question:

(64) ***What/When**** *did the landlord succeed in?*

(67) ***When** should it be the duty of the court to have regard to all the circumstances of the case?*

- admissibility of pseudocleft sentences with the adverbial in the focus position:

(64) ***What/When**** *the landlord succeeded in was establishing elements.*

(67) ***When*** *it should be duty of the court to have regard to all the circumstances of the case is in deciding whether to exercise...*

- inadmissibility of right dislocation constructions:

(64) *The landlord succeeded before the judge in* ***it, establishing***[820G] ***elements (A)(i) and (B).*** (FD)

(67) *It shall be the duty of the court in* ***it*, deciding***[1483G] ***whether to exercise its powers under any of sections 22A to 24BB above and, if so, in what manner*,*** *to have regard to all the circumstances of the case...* (FD)

The preposition *in* in the gerundial semi-clauses (64) and (65) is "automatically selected by the verb... (it is) an appendage to the verb," (Allerton, 1982:60), the verb is prepositional and the *in*-section is assigned "the object-like status of the noun phrase" (Allerton, 1982:61) required by the valency of the verb in question. On the other hand, the gerundial semi-clauses (66) and (67) lie outside the verb valency pattern. They may be regarded as an optional element expressing secondary predication which conveys the notions of accompanying circumstances/time or it may also be time mixed with instrumentality, as demonstrated by an example from Poutsma (*A Grammar of Late Modern English,* 1905:703):

(68) *In so speaking, Rashleigh indeed played a winning card.* (cited in Rudanko, 1996:10)

This interpretation seems plausible in respect of some of the *in*-gerundial adverbials occurring in our corpus:

(69) *... in using*[363G] *the eggshell the tenant is taking*[365V] *advantage of, and making*[366V] *use of, that support.* (CHD)

(70) *... in occupying*[364G] *the eggshell the tenant is taking*[365V] *advantage of, and making*[366V] *use of, that support.* (CHD)

Finally, we should like to comment on the note in the previous paragraph concerning the 'object-like' status of the noun phrase (or the semi-clause in the examples under review) complementing the preposition *in* following the verb *succeed.* Another criterion serving to determine the specific syntactic nature of a prepositional phrase is the passivisation test. If the noun phrase that complements the preposition can be "extracted to become the subject of a passive sentence" (Allerton, 1982:7) it functions as prepositional object, whereas adverbial syntactic function may be assigned to its non-passivisable counterpart, *eg*:

(71) ***Oliver went to the building.* (Allerton, 1982:7) ... *The building was went to by Oliver.* ***

(72) *Oliver objected to the building.* (Allerton, 1982:7) ... *The building was objected to by Oliver.*

Within the syntactic function of object, however, there exists a special variant referred to as *objoid* by Allerton (1982) which

a) cannot passivised, *eg*:

(73) *Oliver referred to the building.* (Allerton, 1982:89) ... *The building was referred to by Oliver.*

(74) *Oliver differed from Charles.* (Allerton, 1982:89) ... *Charles was differred from (by Oliver)**

b) is "not amenable to the '*tough*-movement' transformation" (Allerton, 1982:91), *eg*:

(73) *Oliver referred to the building.* (Allerton, 1982:89) ... *The building was easy to refer to.*

(74) *Oliver differed from Charles.* (Allerton, 1982:89) ... *Charles was easy to differ from.**

Although we did not distinguish between objects and objoids in our syntactic analysis, we realise that there exist finer distinctions within the syntactic function of object. In respect of the object variants, Allerton distinguishes pairs of valency structures comprising them. We will present the respective valency structures which occur in our corpus and exemplify each of them by the matrix verbs as well as instances of the structures:

1. divalent structures (Allerton, 1982:97):

Valency Structure 12: SUBJECT + VERB + OBJECT: (*prevent, consider, admit, avoid*)

(75) *If members of the public who seek to attend cannot be accommodated, the judge* ***should consider adjourning***[1117G] ***the proceedings***[1118DN] *in whole or in part into open court to the extent that this is practical or allowing*[1119G]

one or more representatives of the press to attend the hearing[1120DN] *in chambers.* (FD)

Valency Structure 13: SUBJECT + VERB + OBJOID: (*involve, include*)

(76) *The work* ***includes opening***[437G] ***up the wall*** *between numbers 9 and 11.* (CHD)

Valency Structure 15: SUBJECT + VERB + PREPOSITIONAL OBJECT: (*refer to, agree to*)

(77) *... a court* ***would agree to a term being***[695G] ***included*** *in the new lease that enabled the tenant, or compelled the landlord, to install a floor at the existing*[696Part] *level.* (CHD)

Valency Structure 16: SUBJECT + VERB + PREPOSITIONAL OBJOID: (*relate to, lead to, succeed in, err in*)

(78) *If both elements of that condition are satisfied, then the landlord* ***cannot succeed in establishing***[843G] ***ground (f) of section 30(1) of the Act.*** (CHD)

2. trivalent structures (Allerton, 1982:102):
Valency Structure 125: SUBJECT + VERB + OBJECT + PREPOSITIONAL OBJECT (*leave purpose in*)

(79) *... there must come a point where the necessity of permitting*[846G] *the tenant to undo what the landlord intends* ***would leave so little purpose in the landlord's doing***[847G]***what he intends***... (CHD)

Valency Structure 126: SUBJECT + VERB + OBJECT + PREPOSITIONAL OBJOID (*forgive sb for, prevent sb from, limit sb to, preclude sb from, restrain sb from, deter sb from, prohibit sb from*)

(80) *But even if the subsection does apply to ancillary relief it* ***will not prohibit either party from selling***[1506G] ***the judgment*** *in reliance on the exception provided by section 1(1)(b)(iv)).* (FD)

The last two structures are distinguished on account of the possibility of double passivisation in the former case (other examples may be: *make a mess of, take notice of, lose hope of, pay attention to, take advantage of, make mention of* (CGEL, 1985:1159)).

Double passivisation may be exemplified as follows:

(81a) *Oliver took exception to the proposal.* (Allerton, 1982:110)

(81b) *Exception was taken to the proposal by Oliver.* (Allerton, 1982:110)

(81c) *The proposal was taken exception to by Oliver.* (Allerton, 1982:110)

This double passivisation seems plausible only in respect of example (79) above:

(79a) *... there must come a point where the necessity of permitting*[846G] *the tenant to undo what the landlord intends would leave so little purpose in the landlord's doing*[847G]*what he intends...* (CHD)

(79b) *So little purpose would be left in the landlord's doing what he intends by the necessity...*

(79c) *The landlord's doing what he intends would be left so little purpose in by the necessity...*

In the Valency Structure 126 it is only the object that may be subject to passivisation, *eg*:

(80a) *But even if the subsection does apply to ancillary relief it will not prohibit either party from selling*[1506G] *the judgment in reliance on the exception provided by section 1(1)(b)(iv)).* (FD)

(80b) *Either party will be not prohibited from selling the judgment.*

(80c) *Selling the judgment will not be prohibited from by either party.* *

Regarding the distribution of the valency structures 125 and 126, the latter is more frequent.

Having explained our positions in respect of the particular problematic syntactic interpretations we may proceed to present a tabulated summary showing the results of the syntactic analysis of *-ing* nominalisations occurring in the corpus composed of Law Reports.

Table 2. Distribution of syntactic functions performed by verbal nouns, participles and gerunds in the Law Reports corpus.

	VN	G	Part	Total
Subject	3	4	0	7
Subject complement	1	4	4	9
Prepositional subject complement	1	0	11	12
Prepositional object complement	0	0	8	8
Direct object	7	18	0	25
Prepositional object	1	30+28	0	59
Premodifier	0	91	97	188
Postmodifier	10	100	153	263
Adverbial of accompanying circumstances – time	1	89	84	174
Adverbial of contingency – reason	1	1	3	5
Adverbial of contingency – purpose	0	6	0	6
Adverbial of contingency – result	0	0	4	4
Adverbial of contingency – condition	0	0	4	4
Adverbial of contingency – concession	0	0	5	5
Adverbial of process – manner by comparison	1	0	0	1
Adverbial of process – means	0	20	0	20
Apposition	0	6	0	6
Total	26	397	373	796

As Table 2. shows, the low number of verbal noun occurrence prevents generalisation as to their prevailing syntactic function. In the syntactic functions where verbal nouns compete with gerunds it is the gerund which prevails extensively. For the gerund the main function that it performs in the analysed texts is postmodification (100), followed by premodification (91), adverbial of time (89) and prepositional object (58). Direct object (18) and adverbial of means (20) occur almost equally. The syntactic functions of subject (4) and subject complement (4) are represented, as demonstrated, rather slightly. The rest out of the 19 functions of the gerundial syntactic potential is represented marginally. The participle prevails expectedly as postmodifier (153), exceeding by one third its occurrence as premodifier (97), followed by adverbial of accompanying circumstances/time (84). There are 8 cases of prepositional object complement and 11 cases of prepositional subject complement. In four cases the participle complements the subject without a preposition. The frequency of the rest of the syntactic functions is again quite immaterial. In both the function of postmodifier and premodifier participles outnumber gerunds, in the case of postmodification the ratio is more significant in favour of the participles. Gerundial adverbials, on the other hand, slightly outnumber the participial ones.

The following section is aimed to comment on respective syntactic functions in which verbal nouns, gerunds and participles occur in our texts.

Subject, object.

These syntactic functions are restricted to verbal nouns and gerunds. The **subject** is realised by 3 verbal nouns and 4 gerunds of which 1 takes the passive form. The subject is expressed in 2 cases, one by the possessive pronoun and the other by the common case of a noun.

Looking at the function of **object** the cases of prepositional object (59) outnumber those of direct object (25) more than twice. Both functions are dominated by the gerund. In the category of **direct object** the gerund (18 cases) is in the passive in 1 case, there are no perfect forms of the gerund in this function. The subject is expressed by the possessive case of a noun twice, by the common case of a noun six times, and once by the objective case of the pronoun *it* (*ex* 748), it is unexpressed in 9 cases. The gerundial **prepositional object** (the total of 58 cases) occurs as adjective complementation in 28 cases while in 30 cases it complements verbs, the ratio being almost 1:1, which seems to support the assertion of Biber *et al.* that "*Ing*-clauses following adjectival predicate are most common in academic prose." (Biber *et al.*, 1999:749) There are 3 cases of the passive gerund and one occurrence of the perfect gerund as verbal complementation and 22 cases of the passive gerund as adjective complementation (all of them complementing the adjective *capable of*), the rest being simple gerundial forms. As to the expression of subject, there are 2 cases of the explicit subject of secondary predication being expressed by the possessive case of a noun and 7 cases of the common case of a noun in the verbal complementation, and one case where it is expressed by the possessive pronoun and one by the common case of a noun in the adjective complementation.

Subject complement

There are 9 occurrences of subject complement of which 1 is realised by a verbal noun and the rest by equal occurrence of simple gerundial and participial forms without explicit subjects.

Prepositional subject and object complement

With the exception of 1 C_S conveyed by a verbal noun, the syntactic function of **prepositional object complement** (8) and its passive variant **prepositional subject complement** (11) (the object complement becomes the subject complement in the passive clause, see Supplement Two, p. 40) are performed by participles complementing the preposition *as* following the verbs: *describe, read, treat, recognise, construe, paraphrase, accept, dismiss, point to, call for, rely.* In one case of prepositional subject complement the participle is perfect, and in one case it has a perfect passive form. The prepositional object complement occurs in the simple participial form with one exception of the passive. The subject of all of these forms remains unexpressed due to its explicit occurrence in the matrix clause in the function of subject in case of the prepositional subject complement, and in the function of object for the prepositional object complement. We may demonstrate the structures by the following examples of the prepositional subject complement (82) and prepositional object complement (83):

(82) *Whilst in a lease with no deeming^{142G} provision attached to the rent review clause the provisions as to time can properly be described (as laying^{143Part} down "the administrative procedure or machinery"), the same approach cannot be taken to that part of a clause which contains an express deeming^{144G} provision.:143Part – head of a SemiCl, SemiCl – PrepComp, PrepP – PrepC$_S$* (CHD)

(83) *I would apply the presumption first to construe clause 4(8) (as not amounting^{124Part} to a deeming^{125G} provision)....: 124Part – head of a SemiCl, SemiCl – PrepComp, PrepP – PrepC$_O$* (CHD)

Premodifier

Premodifying syntactic function is performed by gerunds and participles, the ratio being almost 1:1. Gerunds and participles cannot be taken as competing in this syntactic function as there are considerable differences between them: gerundial premodifiers can be paraphrased by a prepositional phrase whereas participial premodifiers correspond to a relative clause, *eg*:

(84) *a letting^{684G} space* (CHD) .... *a space for letting*

(85) *the existing^{413Part} floor* (CHD) .... *the floor which exists*

Distinctions are present also in respect of intonation: falling intonation with the main stress on the first member when the *-ing* form is interpreted gerundially, and the level stress in case of participial premodifiers.

Postmodifier

The postmodifying syntactic function is shared by all three types of *-ing* forms – verbal nouns (10), gerunds (100) and participles (153). The ratio, roughly 1:10:15, shows that the participle outnumbers the gerund 1.5 times in this function with gerunds occurring as prepositional complementations and participles being attached directly to the nominal head.

(86) *I have had [the advantage (of reading*[1401G] *in draft the judgment of Dame Elizabeth Butler-Sloss P.)]: 1401G – head of a SemiCl, SemiCl – PrepComp, PrepP – Postmod in a NP* (FD)

(87) *In the absence of (any express terms specifying*[119Part] *what is to happen in default of the exercise of the rights given to the respective parties within the permitted periods of time,) the presumption applies....:* 119 Part – head of a SemiCl, SemiCl – Postmod in a NP (CHD)

The ratio of verbal nouns to gerunds in this syntactic function is 1:10, the number of verbal noun being slightly higher than its statistic norm for this part of our corpus.

In the postmodifying syntactic function the gerunds occurs after the following prepositions:

Table 3. Prepositions in *-ing* postmodifications.

of	for	in	to	as to	against	at	on	far from	in relation to	for the purpose of	total
41	31	13	11	6	3	1	1	1	1	1	110

As the table shows, the most frequent prepositions are *of* and *for* followed by *in* and *to*, the number of the rest of them being rather marginal in this respect. Heads of these postmodifications are prevailingly abstract nouns denoting concepts. The most frequent heads for the sequence *of* + *-ing* include: *effect* (6), *consequences* (5), *practice* (5), *review* (3), *necessity* (3), *advantage* (3), *doctrine* (2), *object* (2), and one of each of the following *service, benefits, means, danger, desirability, possibility, meaning, purpose, sense, context, convenience, intention.* The most frequent nominal heads for the sequence *for* + *-ing* are: access and *facilities* (8), *reason/s* (5), *provision* (3), *step*/s (2), *grounds* (2), *procedure/s* (2), *machinery* (2) and one of each of the following: *repair, basis, guidelines, device, entry, justification, rules*. The sequence *in* + *-ing* is preceded by *notice* (3), *consent* (3), *difficulty* (2), *interest* (2), *delay* (1), *function* (1), *practice* (1). In the sequence *to* + *-ing* the preposition *to* seems to correspond with the valency pattern of the original verb as it follows nouns derived from verbs: *reference/s* (5), *objection* (4), *agreement* (1), *contribution* (1).

Participial postmodifiers modify nominal heads which denote abstract as well as concrete items, both animate and inanimate.

From among the morphological forms of gerunds and participles, the perfect aspect is excluded in this syntactic function (see Supplement Two, p.52). There are 4 passive gerunds and 2 passive participles in this function. The subject of gerundial postmodification is expressed explicitly in 22 cases, all of them by the common case of a noun except for one occurrence of *there*. The subject of participial postmodification is the head of the noun phrase it postmodifies.

Adverbials

The function of adverbials is performed by the gerund and participle in this part of the corpus, leaving aside the three cases of its verbal noun implementation. The ratio of gerundial and participial occurrence in this function is 1.1 : 1, which is again almost identical. Table 2, Chapter Three (p. 139) shows the following data:

Table 4. Adverbial syntactic function of *-ing* forms.

VN	G	P	Total
3	116	100	219

Out of the potential of semantic roles conveyed by these adverbials, (as tabulated in Supplement Two, p. 54), the following were found in the analysed texts: time (174), reason (5), purpose (6), result (4), condition (4), concession (5), manner by comparison (1), means (20). As can be seen, it is primarily the adverbial of time and time-related accompanying circumstances which is the dominating adverbial syntactic function performed by the gerund and participle in our texts.

Adverbials of accompanying circumstances – time (174 cases) are expressed by gerunds and participles with almost equal share *ie* 89 gerunds to 84 participles (beside 1 verbal noun). Gerundial adverbials occur after the following prepositions *without* (53), *in* (28), *before* (5), *with* (2), *after* (1). As can be seen, gerundial semi-clause constructions are in all their occurrences introduced by (and also recognised as being gerundial by reference to their complementation of) a preposition, the most frequent of them being *without.* At the same time, these are the only prepositions used to introduce time framework of gerundial action in relation to the matrix clause. The range and frequency of conjunctions introducing participial adverbials of time is much more limited, they occur only after the conjunctions *when* (10), *while* (5), the rest (69) being attached asyndetically.

There are 4 passive gerundial forms and 1 passive perfect gerund, 8 perfect and 5 passive participial forms and 2 passive perfect participles. Common case of a noun as subject occurs 5 times with the gerund and 7 times with the participle. The pronoun *it* occurs twice with the gerund, in both its objective and possessive forms; there are 2 occurrences of *there* subject and one case of the pronoun *the others* as subject with the participle.

Adverbials of contingency – the total of 24 contingency cases is distributed among the adverbials of **reason** (5), **purpose** (6), **result** (4), **condition** (4), **concession** (5). The adverbials of result, condition and concession are expressed by simple participial forms, without explicit subjects. Purpose is conveyed by simple gerundial forms following the preposition *for* or its complex variant *for the purpose of,* without an explicit subject as well. There is one adverbial of reason in the form of verbal noun occurring after the PP preposition *by reason of,* one simple gerundial adverbial following *for* and three participial adverbials of reason joined asyndetically, two of which occur in the passive perfect with the objective case of the pronoun *it* and one occurs in a simple form with the subject *that.*

Adverbials of process – we found one example of **manner** adverbial (manner by comparison) expressed by a verbal noun and 20 cases of simple gerundial adverbials of **means** with the exception of one case of the passive gerund with the subject conveyed by the common case of a noun. In one case the subject is realised by the possessive pronoun. All the gerundial forms complement the preposition *by.*

Apposition

There are 6 cases of simple gerunds without explicit subjects which are apposited to a noun for explanatory purposes.

The following tables summarise the occurrence of respective forms of gerunds and participles (Table 5.) and the mode of conveying the subject thereof (Table 6.).

Table 5. Aspect and voice contrast variants of gerunds and participles.

Kind of form	Gerund	Participle
Simple active	359	351
Simple passive	36	8
Perfect active	1	9
Perfect passive	1	5
Total of forms	397	373

As demonstrated in Table 5., both the gerund and the participle are implemented basically by their simple variants. The ratio of simple forms to non-simple forms is 9:1 for the gerunds and 16:1 for the participles. Out of 36 passive gerundial forms 22 function as adjective complementation following the preposition *of.* Eight out of nine perfect participles and five out of eight passive participles occur as adverbials of accompanying circumstances/time. The rest of the frequency numbers seems rather immaterial.

Table 6. Explicit and implicit subjects of gerunds and participles.

Kind of subject	Gerund	Participle
Noun – possessive case	4	0
Noun – common case	42	6
Personal pronoun – possessive case	4	0
Personal pronoun – objective case	2	2
Other types of pronouns	1	4
Total of explicit subject	53	12
Total of implicit subject	344	361
Total of *-ing* forms	397	373

Table 6. makes clear that the common case of nouns is by far the most frequent means of expressing the subject of *-ing* forms required by the attachment rule, which supports the research carried out by Biber *et al.* "The objective case is used for the overwhelming majority (over 90 %) of noun phrases occurring in the pattern verb + NP + *-ing* clause." (Biber *et al.*, 1999:750) The structures with the common case of a noun and objective case of a pronoun functioning as the subject are deemed to be absolute gerundial or participial constructions. As can be noticed, we identified 45 absolute gerundial constructions and 12 absolute participial constructions. There are 8 cases where the subject of a gerund is in the possessive case – 4 nouns and 4 pronouns, (the possessive case is obviously excluded in regard of the participle). This finding only supports what was suggested before, *ie* that the possessive case seems to be a rather formal variant giving way to the common case/objective case, both being semantically equivalent, compare (88) and (89), (90) and (91) where the sentential context is almost identical, *eg*:

(88) *Were it otherwise it would involve a **tenant's** being^{654G} able to say: '...some entirely different entity.': 654G – head of a SemiCl, SemiCl –* O_D (CHD)

(89) *It would involve the **landlord** having^{235G} to serve a notice, in effect asking the tenant if it wanted to serve a counter-notice...: 235G – head of a SemiCl, SemiCl –* O_D *(absolute construction)* (CHD)

(90) *There must, however, in my judgment, come a point where the necessity of permitting^{588G} the tenant to undo what the landlord intends would leave so little purpose (in the **landlord's** doing^{589G} what he intends) that he could*

not reasonably do that which he otherwise intends without possession.: 589G – head of a SemiCl, SemiCl – PrepComp, PrepP – O_{Prep} (CHD)

(91) *The judge thought that there came a point where the necessity of permitting*[934G] *the tenant to undo what the landlord intends to do would leave so little purpose (in* ***the landlord*** *doing*[935G] *what he intends to do)....: 935G – head of a SemiCl, SemiCl – PrepComp, PrepP –* O_{Prep} *(absolute construction)* (CHD)

The personal pronoun *it* as subject occurs in both its possessive and objective forms, *eg*:

(92) *Conceding*[518Part] *that the work is a 'substantial work of construction', that is not inconsistent (with* ***its*** *being*[519G] *a necessary repair for the carrying*[52VN1] *out of which the landlord was entitled to access in terms of the leases).: 519G – head of a SemiCl, SemiCl – PrepComp, PrepP –* O_{Prep} (CHD)

(93) *... to obtain possession the landlord has to terminate the current tenancy (without* ***it*** *being*[547G] *followed by a new tenancy.): 547 passive G – head of a SemiCl, SemiCl – PrepComp, PrepP – Adv of accomp/time (absolute construction)* (CHD)

Comparing above examples, i.e. (88) and (89), (90) and (91) for nouns and (92) and (93) for pronouns, we would like to show that the formality of style is neither strengthened nor weakened by the use of either form of the subject, as both seem to be stylistically as well as semantically equivalent (examples above were taken from direct as well as indirect speech and the two of the forms were used interchangeably, or, at least, we could not reveal any satisfactory substantiation of the particular choices).

The rest of the gerundial (344) and participial constructions (361) occur without the explicit subject, great majority of them complying with the attachment rule. Adverbial *-ing* forms show quite a high frequency of the so called dangling form, *ie* "a non-finite circumstantial *-ing* clause with an understood subject that differs from that of the main clause." (Biber *et al.*, 1999:829) 28 out of 116 adverbial gerunds (which is almost every fourth adverbial gerund) and 42 out of 100 circumstantial participles (which is almost every second adverbial participle) may be classified as unattached forms, the omission of the explicit subject implying a general agent of the action specified by the *-ing* form, or the implied subject is to be identified with *I, we,* and *you* of the writer, *eg*:

(94) *(Before turning[27G] to consider the law), it is necessary to set out briefly the facts of this case which were not the subject of dispute.: 27G – head of a SemiCl, SemiCl – PrepComp, PrepP – Adv of accomp/time (dangling gerundial construction)* (CHD)

(95) *Thus the issue of whether such a provision would be a sufficient "contraindication" to rebut the general presumption that time was not of the essence (in construing[64G] such clauses) was not directly considered.: 64G – head of a SemiCl, SemiCl – PrepComp, PrepP – Adv of accomp/time (dangling gerundial construction)* (CHD)

(96) *Having[139Part] reviewed at length the various authorities, it is necessary to form a view as to the correct approach to a deeming[140G] provision in a rent review clause in the light of those authorities.: 139 perfect Part – head of a SemiCl, SemiCl – Adv of accomp/time (dangling participial construction)* (CHD)

(97) *The ground relied on was that set out in section 30(1)(f) of the 1954 Act and the issue before the judge was therefore whether that ground was satisfied, having[338Part] regard to the terms of that subsection and the terms of section 31A of the 1954 Act.: 338Part – head of a SemiCl, SemiCl – Adv of accomp/time (dangling participial construction)* (CHD)

This may support the observations of Dušková that these forms are a rather frequent means in scientific writing and that they are not felt as objectionable.

Summing it up, in the present part of our research we analysed a corpus of 51 614 words consisting of the wording of three judgments published in the 2002 Law Reports by the Incorporated Council of Law Reporting (Chancery Division of the High Court of Justice, 305 – 364, and the Family Division of the High Court of Justice, 261-311), UK (ranking with the stylistic layer of application of law). We identified the total of 1558 *-ing* forms of which 796 were subject to analysis in respect of syntactic functions (26 verbal nouns, 397 gerunds and 373 participles).

Table 2, Chapter Three shows that the prevailing syntactic function in all of the three analysed categories of condensers is that of postmodification (10 verbal nouns, 100 gerunds, 153 participles). The rest of the 16 verbal noun cases is distributed among the functions of subject, subject complement, object and adverbials. As far as the range of syntactic functions concerns, the basic difference between the gerund and participle rests in the gerundial potential to perform the syntactic functions of subject (4), prepositional object (58), direct object (18). As was mentioned, postmodification dominates the repertory of gerundial syntactic functions (100), followed by almost equal occurrence of premodification (91) and adverbial of accompanying circumstances/time (89). Among the rest of the adverbial semantic roles of the gerund, it is process – means that occurs 20 times. There are three principal syntactic functions of the participle in the analysed texts: the above-mentioned postmodification (153 cases), premodification (97 cases), and adverbial of accompanying circumstances/time (84 cases). In the adverbial syntactic function gerunds and participles do not display semantic distinctions. It might be therefore argued that it is the stylistic factor which influences the choice of a particular item, *ie* more nominal gerundial semi-clause introduced by a preposition or less nominal participial semi-clause attached mostly asyndetically.

As for the structural forms of gerunds and participles, we found that both occur prevailingly in their simple forms (359 out of 397 gerunds and 351 out of 373 participles), with almost every tenth gerund occurring in the passive, and only three per cent of the passive and perfect participial forms. 13 % of the gerundial constructions and 3 % of the participial constructions occur with the explicit subject, mostly the form of the common case of nouns.

CHAPTER FOUR
Evaluation of the syntactic analyses of Acts of Parliament and Law Reports – comparison

In this Chapter we should like to comment on the hypothesis set forth in the introductory part of our thesis. It consisted in the assertion that the texts of judgments ranked with the stylistic layer of application of law are less nominal in character than the wording of the Acts of Parliament ranked with the stylistic layer of legislation that we analysed on similar lines in the first half of the research. We expected this to be demonstrated by the following parameters, supported by the research data:

- higher number of participial occurrence,
- lower ratio of verbal noun *vs* gerundial occurrence,
- lower occurrence of *-ing* forms as complements of prepositions.

The output data of both analyses may be summarised as follows:

Table 1. Outcome of Acts of Parliament and Law Reports syntactic analyses of *-ing* forms.

	Acts of Parliament	Law Reports
Total of words	51 769	51 614
Total of *-ing* forms	1 554	1 558
Total of condensers	925	796
Verbal nouns	82	26
Gerunds	446	397
Participles	397	373

First observation which seemed rather surprising was the fact that in both corpora, comprising more than 51 500 words each, we identified almost equal number of *-ing* forms, *ie* approximately 1550, which makes 3 % of the total. Out of these forms, there were 925 analysed condensers in the Acts of Parliament and 796 analysed condensers in the Law Reports. Proceeding to the respective types of condensers we found that the first and the second part of our hypothesis proved true, namely the higher relative frequency of participles and the lower occurrence of verbal nouns in the Law Reports.

Out of the total of condensers, the percentage of participial occurrence makes 47 % in the Law Reports and 43 % in the Acts of Parliament, the difference being 4 %. Although the actual number of participial occurrence is lower in the former corpus, its proportional value increased.

We were also right in the assumption concerning the ratio of verbal noun to gerundial frequency of occurrence. In the Acts of Parliament the ratio was 1:6, whereas in the Law Reports it was 1:15 which is still higher than that found by Marková in the fiction, *ie* 1:20 (Marková, 1986:85). These decreasing numbers show that the stylistic factor counts in respect of the selection of verbal noun *vs* gerund.

The frequency findings which imply a somewhat peripheral position of the verbal noun against the gerund, however, should not be taken as showing that the verbal noun is a form that is in retreat. This language means, which was once a source form for all of the current *-ing* realisations, preserved its original nominal force and is still used in the contexts where the first valency slot (agent) of the verbal base is conceived as loosened although processual implications are retained by the form. If we compare the non-*ing* verbal noun, *-ing* verbal noun and gerund in this respect the following may be the result:

Table 2. Semantic features of the non-*ing* verbal noun, *-ing* verbal noun and gerund.

	non-*ing* verbal noun	*-ing* verbal noun	gerund
agential implications	----	----	+
Processuality implied	----	+	+
factitiveness implied	+	----	+

The following extracts from the British Nationality Act 1981 may be used to demonstrate that a) there exist three separate types, b) the *-ing* ending is used to form derivatives on the level of abstract nominalisations, *ie* the gap-filling function of the *-ing* ending, and c) the *-ing* verbal nouns are processual in contrast with the non-*ing* verbal nouns.

(1) *41. – (1) The Secretary of State may by regulations make provision generally for **carrying into effect** the purposes of this Act, in particular provision –*
*a) for **prescribing** anything which under this Act is to be prescribed;*
*c) for the **registration** of anything required or authorised by or under this Act to be registered;*
*d) for the **administration** and **taking** of oath of allegiance under this Act, as to the time within which oaths of allegiance must be taken, and for the **registration of oaths** of allegiance;*
*f) for the **cancellation** of the registration of, and the **cancellation** and amendment of certificates of naturalisation relating to, persons deprived of citizenship under this Act, and for **requiring** such certificates to be delivered up for those purposes;*
*i) for **enabling** the births and deaths of British citizens, British Dependent Territories citizens, British Overseas citizens, British subjects and British protected persons born or dying in any country in which Her Majesty's government in the United Kingdom has for the time being no diplomatic or*

consular representatives to be registered – ... (British Nationality Act 1981, section 41(1))

(2) *41. – (2) The Secretary of State may with the consent of the Treasury by regulations make provision for the* ***imposition, recovery*** *and* ***application*** *of fees in connection with any of the following matters, namely –*
b) the ***effecting*** *in the United Kingdom of any registration authorised by or under this Act;*
c) the ***making*** *in the United Kingdom of any declaration, the grant there of any certificate, or the taking there of any oath of allegiance authorised to be made, granted or taken by or under this Act;*
d) the ***supplying*** *in the United Kingdom of a certified or other copy of any notice, certificate, order, declaration or entry given, granted or made under or by virtue of this Act or any of the former nationality Acts;*
e) the ***carrying*** *out of searches in or of any registers or other records, being registers or records held in the United Kingdom by or on behalf of the Secretary of State, which are or may be relevant for the purpose of determining the status of any person under this Act or any of the former nationality Acts;*
f) the ***supplying*** *by or on behalf of the Secretary of State of an opinion in writing concerning the status of any person under this Act or any of the former nationality Acts, or a certified or other copy of such an opinion.* (British Nationality Act, 1981, section 41(2))

Lack of the element of factitiveness with the *-ing* verbal noun may account for the impossibility to derive this form from the non-action verbs while the gerund can be formed from any verbal base, except for the modals. In our opinion, despite the low frequency of the verbal noun its use seems to be justified especially in the contexts that require processuality combined with the possibility to push the agent of the original verbal action away from the centre of attention. This is also supported by the fact that so called attachment rule does not obtain in relation to the verbal nouns; their agent may, if necessary, be expressed explicitly (by *of*-postmodification or *by*-phrase) or it does not have to be expressed at all without it being felt objectionable. As the genre of legislation frequently requires this particular combination of semantic elements, the verbal nouns are rather frequent here. Other way round, should the frequency data (considered in isolation from the semantic, structural and functional implications) be the only factor accountable for a peripheral position of a certain language phenomenon, then for example the participle functioning as the main verb in a complex finite verb phrase would also be in retreat as its frequency is around 30 in both the corpora.

The last of the three assumptions may be tested by comparing the data obtained from the syntactic analyses of the whole corpus. For readers convenience, we supply the outcome data of both analyses in one table below:

Table 3. Summary of the syntactic functions performed by the *-ing* nominalisations occurring in the Acts of Parliament and the Law Reports.

	Verbal noun AP / LR	Gerund AP / LR	Participle AP / LR
Subject	14 / 3	2 / 4	0 / 0
Subject complement	0 / 1	0 / 4	0 / 4
Prepositional subject complement	0 / 1	2 / 0	33 / 11
Prepositional object complement	0 / 0	0 / 0	3 / 8
Direct object	4 / 7	6 / 18	0 / 0
Prepositional object	6 / 1	45 / 58	0 / 0
Premodifier	0 / 0	191 / 91	57 / 97
Postmodifier	19 / 10	76 / 100	287 / 153
Adverbial of place	0 / 0	0 / 0	1 / 0
Adverbial of accompanying circumstances/time	23 / 1	64 / 89	11 / 84
Adverbial of contingency – reason	2 / 1	4 / 1	1 / 3
Adverbial of contingency – purpose	2 / 0	23 / 6	0 / 0
Adverbial of contingency – result	0 / 0	0 / 0	0 / 4
Adverbial of contingency – condition	0 / 0	1 / 0	2 / 4
Adverbial of contingency – concession	0 / 0	0 / 0	2 / 5
Adverbial of process – manner by comparison	1 / 1	4 / 0	0 / 0
Adverbial of means	6 / 0	25 / 20	0 / 0
Adverbial of respect	4 / 0	2 / 0	0 / 0
Adverbial of except	0 / 0	1 / 0	0 / 0
Apposition	1 / 0	0 / 6	0 / 0
Total	82 / 26	446 / 397	397 / 373

In both corpora the syntactic functions shared by the verbal nouns and gerunds are dominated by the latter form, except for the subject in the Acts of Parliament. Among the syntactic functions from which the participles are excluded it is the prepositional object that seems to be most frequently realised by the gerund in both corpora.

Comparing the gerund and the participle, the number of gerunds slightly exceeds that of participles in both cases but the occurrence of the latter shows a proportional increase in the Law Reports corpus, as stated above. There is a special participial performance of the function of prepositional subject and object complement in our texts following the preposition *as* after the verbs such as *regard, treat, consider etc*.

Gerundial and participial premodifiers and postmodifiers do not represent competitive pairs as the semantic and structural nature of both variants is specific. Premodification is represented by 248 cases dominated by the gerund in the Acts of Parliament and 188 cases dominated by the participle in the Law Reports. Postmodification is the principal syntactic function for both forms in both corpora in respect of frequency. What seems interesting is an unexpected proportional increase of gerundial over participial postmodifiers in the Law Reports. The ratio was 1:4 in the Acts of Parliament and only 1:1,5 in the Law Reports (gerund : participle) which means that in the Law Reports almost every second postmodification is gerundial *ie* complementing a preposition while in the Acts of Parliament it is only every fourth.

We may speak of true competition of gerundial and participial forms if we look at the adverbial syntactic function. In the Acts of Parliament the ratio of gerundial *versus* participial performance of this function was 7:1. In the Law Reports the same ratio was 1,2 :1, thus while the number of gerunds in this function was almost the same in both corpora (124 in the AP, 116 in the LR), the number of participles is almost six times higher in the Law Reports (17 in the AP, 100 in the LR).

Generally, it may be argued that while the gerund in the adverbial syntactic function always complements a preposition the participial adverbials tend to be attached without any connective means. For example if we take the syntactic function of time adverbial in both parts of the corpus the gerundial performance was introduced by one of the following prepositions *in* (35/28), *without* (12/53), *on* (8/0), *before* (6/5), *after* (3/1) or *with* (0/2). The prevailing mode of joining participial time adverbials with the matrix clause was asyndetical (10/69) (the only conjunctions used in the corpus were *when* (1/10) and *while* (0/5)). The number of participial time adverbials increased in the second part of the corpus by almost eight times (11/84).

The last assumption of our hypothesis, namely the lower frequency of *-ing* forms as complements of prepositions in the stylistic layer of application of law also proved true because although we actually detected increasing occurrence of the prepositional variants of object, postmodification and adverbial realised by the gerund (and the verbal noun) in the corpus made of Law Reports the total of *-ing* forms complementing a preposition was still lower in the Law Reports than in the Acts of Parliament, *ie* AP 346 : LR 309. On the other hand, we identified six-times more frequent occurrence of the participle in the function of adverbial, as mentioned in the above paragraph.

As for the morphological variants of the gerunds and participles, Table 4. below should enable a numeric comparison of the respective forms of condensers in both kinds of texts. We may see that there is no significant difference between the corpora in this respect. It seems clear that both the gerund and the participle occur predominantly in their simple forms. Out of the rest of the forms it is only the passive that has almost 10 %-gerundial occurrence in the Law Reports. Perfect forms occur rather marginally.

Table 4. Aspect and voice contrast variants of gerunds and participles.

Kind of form	Gerund AP / LR	Participle AP / LR
Simple active	426 / 359	386 / 351
Simple passive	14 / 36	5 / 8
Perfect active	3 / 1	4 / 9
Perfect passive	3 / 1	2 / 5
Total of forms	446 / 397	397 / 373

Table 5. Explicit and implicit subjects of gerunds and participles.

Kind of subject	Gerund AP / LR	Participle AP / LR
Noun – possessive case	0 / 4	0 / 0
Noun – common case	8 / 42	1 / 6
Personal pronoun – poss. case	10 / 4	0 / 0
Personal pronoun – obj. case	0 / 2	0 / 2
Other types of pronouns	1 / 1	0 / 4
Total of explicit subject: 85	19 / 53 72	1 / 12 13
Total of implicit subject: 1528	427 / 344 771	396 / 361 757
Total of gerunds and participles: 1613	446 / 397 843	397 / 373 770

Table 5. above surveys the occurrence of explicit and implicit subjects of the action conveyed by the gerund or participle, and shows that in the examined corpus gerunds and participles prevail without the explicit subject (the ratio is 18:1, *ie* 1528 implicit *vs* 85 explicit).

As can be seen, it is the gerund that takes the explicit subject more frequently in both types of the analysed texts (almost 6:1). In the gerundial cases where the choice is between the common case form and the possessive form, the former prevails. A general observation that the possessive case seems to be a rather formal variant giving way to the common case/objective case seems to be less applicable in respect of the Acts of Parliaments sub-genre, where personal pronouns occur exclusively in the possessive case and nouns in the common case which might be viewed as a genre-specific feature, both forms being identical as to the level of formality.

Corpus analysis results regarding the occurrence of absolutes have been summarised below:

Table 6. Gerundial vs. participial absolutes – corpus findings

	Acts of Parliament	Law Reports	Total
Gerundial absolutes	9	45	54
Participial absolutes	1	12	13
Total	10	57	67

As Table 6 shows we identified 67 cases of absolutes in the whole corpus. The ratio of gerundial to participial absolutes is about 1 to 4 in favour of the gerunds in the whole corpus. Gerundial absolutes dominate as postmodification, participial absolutes as adverbial modifiers, especially accompanying circumstances of time. The nominal subject extensively prevails over the pronominal one. As for a genre comparison, absolutes are preferred in the Law Reports. This might be explained by the fact that the texts of Acts of Parliament generally tend to be more impersonal, general, and thus more flexible in respect of its universal applicability. Their authors seem to avoid explicit subjects of secondary predication, as these are implicitly present as authoritative source/agency of the original verbal action.

Of 771 gerundial and 757 participial constructions with implicit agents (Table 5, total of 1528), a great majority complies with the attachment rule. Nevertheles, both texts also show a rather frequent occurrence of dangling forms, *ie* the structures that function as adverbials and do not comply with the attachment rule. The omission of the subject in most cases implies the author or general agent or the agent is present in the matrix clause in the function other than that of the subject of the finite verb. In the Acts of Parliament it is almost every third adverbial gerund and participle that is dangling while in the Law Reports it is every fourth adverbial gerund and almost every second adverbial participle that is unattached. We may, thus, assert that legal English seems to favour this kind of construction (at least in its legislative and law-reporting sub-gcnres). We assume that they are not considered defective as they do not cause any problems in identifying the proper agent of the - *ing* action, but on the contrary, they seem to be rather standard structural variants of gerundial and participial condensers.

CONCLUSION

In order to fulfil the aims set forth in the introductory passage, we should like to complete this study by repeating the basic tenets of our approach to the issue of *-ing* forms and summarising the conditioning factors influencing the selection of a particular type of condenser.

The current inventory of *-ing* forms in English represents a scalar spectre whose members cline from the full nominality (deverbal noun) to the full verbality (participle as the main verb of a complex finite verb phrase) with an intermediate stage (verbal noun, gerund and participle functioning as condensers), representing gradience between the two of the statuses. The concept of gradience is central in respect of the *-ing* forms ranked with condensers as it is inherently present in the account of their semantic, morphological and syntactic characteristics. It is also reflected in the status of the *-ing* ending which seems to have developed into a multifunctional means capable of forming fully nominal and verbal items as well as items which are gradient between them. In this respect its status is conceived as grading from the full derivationality towards the full inflectionality with an intermediate grade where the tests show transition from derivation to inflection. All of these aspects have been examined in order to arrive at a uniform word-class assignment to be applied to particular *-ing* representations occurring in our corpus.

The overall synchronic approach is accompanied with a brief diachronic outline of the origination of these forms. The reason for the existence of distinct combinations of verbo-nominal properties expressed by formally identical items is the fact that they have developed from the common source – a denominal Old English suffix – which has gradually extended its nominal functional scope. The shift of the syntactic function of the items thereby formed has brought about the changes on the semantic, morphological and syntactic levels and resulted in the formation of the current scalar spectre of the *-ing* forms.

The extended syntactic functional scope has brought on a competition of the available types of *-ing* forms. Summary of the factors conditioning the choice of a particular type of condenser in the syntactic functions shared by several items has been set forth as one of the aims of our research. On the grounds of approximately 1700 examined *-ing* condensers out of the total of more than 3000 *-ing* forms occurring in the analysed legal English corpus (represented by two genres of legal English, namely Acts of Parliament and Law Reports), we should like supply the following conditioning factors:

- **semantic** *ie* selection is always primarily concerned with the semantics of the immediate sentential context which may require specific combinations of semantic features (agential implication, processuality, factitiveness, abstractness, concreteness *etc*). It was demonstrated that an inappropriate interpretation of the syntactic and structural status of a particular *-ing* form may result in an undesired semantic shift.

- **morphological** *ie* selection is necessitated by formal requirements – inadmissibility of a certain form of subject, necessity to express the category of definiteness, attempt to avoid passivisation, supporting certain syntactic interpretation of the construction, anaphoric reference to be conveyed by *t/hereof*, lack of non-*ing* verbal noun variant *etc.*
- **functional** *ie* sentential context and communicative purpose may require that the *-ing* construction may perform denotative or predicative functions.
- **stylistic** *ie* overall character of a particular genre may favour certain variants *eg* prepositional variants, types that suppress agential implications *etc*; another relevant stylistic feature seems to be a desired co-ordination of items that are structurally uniform. In order to include this factor into the list it seemed necessary to compare distinct genres (in the present research the legislation and judicial decisions) available in a particular discourse (here legal language). This approach may be supported by the following citation: "We are, of course, dealing here with grammatical facts of a 'more or less' rather than 'all or nothing' kind. This is precisely the reason for resorting to the painstaking task of counting occurrences and producing contingency tables. The results seem to demonstrate that such procedure can highlight tendencies of interest not only in synchronic and diachronic linguistics but in stylistics and literary studies; and that, in consequence, far more extensive inquiries on these lines would be clearly rewarding." (Quirk, 1995:111)

The factor to be placed on the top of the above list is the fact that the valency ties of the original verb seem to have loosened in the direction to the bottom of the list below which has reflected in the semantic, structural and syntactic levels related to the respective types of nominalisations in question:

participle as main verb of a complex finite verb phrase

participle as condenser

gerund

verbal noun

non-*ing* verbal noun

deverbal noun.

SUMMARY

The submitted study was concerned with the issue of *-ing* nominalisations in both the theoretical aspect (delimitation of respective types) and practical aspect (survey of their corpus occurrence). We concentrated on the syntactic functions of those that serve as sentence condensers *ie* verbal noun, gerund, participle.

The research was presented in the following sections:

In Chapter One we attempted to solve the issue of word-class assignment in respect of the existing types of *-ing* forms. We evaluated the status of the *-ing* ending, outlined the origination of the *-ing* spectre and delimited syntactic borderlines between particular constructions, along with the account of the semantic, morphological and syntactic potential of *-ing* forms.

In Chapter Two we explained the concept of legal language, genre stratification of legal language and we attempted to characterise the genres of legislation and judicial decisions, the samples of which formed our corpus: Family Law Act 1996, Theft Act 1968, and three judgments published in the 2002 Law Reports by the Incorporated Council of Law Reporting (Chancery Division of the High Court of Justice, 305 – 364, and the Family Division of the High Court of Justice, 261-311), UK. We further described the method of syntactic analysis and exemplified the occurrence of target *-ing* forms, based on a detailed syntactic analysis of the corpus (the length of approximately 100 000 words, total of more than 3000 *-ing* forms, more than half of them were the target condensers).

In Chapter Three we tabulated and evaluated the data based on the syntactic analysis of the Law Reports corpus. We found that the *-ing* condensers prevail in the syntactic functions of postmodification, premodification and adverbial modifier.

In Chapter Four we attempted to compare the results of the syntactic analyses of both parts of our legal English corpus *ie* legislation and judgments.

The final generalising conclusions grounded in the research consisted in a scalar outline of options to express the verb-related meaning by the *-ing* nominalisations and summarising the conditioning factors which influence the selection of a particular type of condensers.

BIBLIOGRAPHY

Adams, V. 1973. *An introduction to Modern English Word-formation*. London: Longman.

Austin, J. L. 1962. *How to Do Things With Words*. Oxford.

Alerton, D. J. 1982. *Valency and the English Verb*. London: Academic Press INC (London).

Bauer, L. 1983. *English Word-Formation*. Cambridge: CUP.

Bauer, L. 2003. *Introducing Linguistic Morphology*. 2nd edition. Edinburgh: Edinburgh University Press.

Baugh, A. C. 1957. *A History of the English Language*. Englewood Cliffs: Prentice-Hall, Inc.

Bhatia, V. K. 1993. *Analysing Genre. Language Used in Professional Settings*. Longman: London and New York.

Bhatia, V. K., Swales J. M. 1983. An approach to the Linguistic Study of Legal Documents. In: *Fachsprache* 5/3, Wien, pp. 98 – 109.

Biber, D., *et al.* 1999. *Longman Grammar of Spoken and Written English*. Harlow: Pearson Education Limited.

Bolinger, D. 1975. *Aspects of language*. New York: Harcourt Brace Jovanovich, Inc.

British Nationality Act 1981. London: Her Majesty's Stationary Office.

Brown Corpus. 1979.

Charrow, V. R., *et al.* 1982. Characteristics and Functions of Legal Language. In: *Sublanguage: Studies in Restricted Semantic Domains*. Berlin/New York: Walter de Gruyter.

Chartrand, M. *et al.* 1997. *English for Contract and Company Law*. London: Sweet and Maxwell Limited.

Chomsky, N. 1970. Remarks On Nominalizations. In: *Readings in English Transformational Grammar*, Ginn and Company, Waltham, Mass., 184 – 221.

Chromá, M. 2003. *New Introduction to Legal English. Díl. I and II.* Praha: Karolinum.

Colen, A. 1984. *A Syntactic and Semantic Study of English Predicative Nominals*. Brussels: Koninklijke Academie.

Craies, W.F. 1971. *A Treatise on statute law*. London: Sweet and Maxwell Limited.

Cross, R. 1968. *Precedent in English law*. The Clarendon Press: Oxford.

Cruse, A. 2004. *Meaning in Language*. Oxford: Oxford University Press.

Crystal, D. 1995. *The Cambridge Encyclopedia of the English Language*. Cambridge: CUP.

Crystal, D. Davy, D. 1969. *Investigating English Style*. London: Longman.

Curme, G.O. 1979. *A Grammar of the English Language.* Volume II. Essex, Connecticut: VERBATIM.
Curme, G. O. 1980. *A Grammar of the English Language.* Volume I. Essex, Connecticut: VERBATIM.
Danet, B. 1980. Language in the legal process. In: *Law and Society Review,* Vol. 14, No. 3, pp. 445 – 564.
Danet, B. 1984. Legal Discourse. In: *Text. An Interdisciplinary Journal for the Study of Discourse.* Amsterdam: Mouton.
Danet B. 1985. Legal Discourse. In: *Handbook of Discourse Analysis.* Vol. 1. London: Academic Press INC.
Dušková, L. 1988. *Mluvnice současné angličtiny na pozadí češtiny.* Praha: SPN.
Dušková, L. 1999a. *Studies in the English Language*, Part 1. Praha: Karolinum – Charles University Press.
Dušková, L. 1999b. *Studies in the English Language*, Part 2. Praha: Karolinum – Charles University Press.
Dušková, L. 2002. *Syntax současné angličtiny.* Karolinum: Praha.
Family Law Act 1996. London: Her Majesty's Stationary Office.
Ferenčík, M. 2002. *The Structure of English. A Coursebook of English Grammar.* Part 1. Bratislava: Creativ line.
Firbas, J. 1961. On the Communicative Value of the Modern English Finite Verb. In: *Brno Studies in English,* 3:79 – 102.
Firbas, J. 1992. *Functional Sentence Perspective in Written and Spoken Communication,* CUP: Cambridge.
Fotion, N. 1971. Master Speech Acts. In: *The Philosophical Quarterly.* Vol. 21. The University of St. Andrews.
Fraser, B. 1970. Some Remarks on the Action Nominalization in English. *Readings in English Transformational Grammar*, Mass.: Ginn.
Gove, P.B. 1965. "Gerund/Noun" and "Participle/Adjective". In: *American Speech,* 40:40 – 46.
Greenbaum, S.(1973. Adverbial *-Ing* Participle Constructions in English. In: *Anglia,* 91:1 – 10.
Hais, K. 1991. *Anglická gramatika.* Bratislava: SPN.
Hladký, J. 1961. Remarks on Complex Condensation Phenomena in Some English and Czech Contexts. In: *Brno Studies in English,* 3:105 – 118.
Horecký, J. 1994. Semantics of derived words. In: *Acta Facultatis Philosophicae Universitatis Šafarikanae.* Prešov: FF UPJŠ Košice.
Janigová, S., Vargová, B. 2001. *Introduction to Legal English for Students of the Law Faculty UPJŠ in Košice.* Košice : UPJŠ.
Jespersen, O. 1965a. *A Modern English Grammar on Historical Principles.* Part I. London – Copenhagen: George Allen and Unwin LTD – Ejnar Munksgaad.

Jespersen, O. 1965b. *A Modern English Grammar on Historical Principles.* Part II. London – Copenhagen: George Allen and Unwin LTD – Ejnar Munksgaad.
Jespersen, O. 1965c. *A Modern English Grammar on Historical Principles.* Part III. London – Copenhagen: George Allen and Unwin LTD – Ejnar Munksgaad.
Jespersen, O. 1965d. *A Modern English Grammar on Historical Principles.* Part IV. London – Copenhagen: George Allen and Unwin LTD – Ejnar Munksgaad.
Jespersen, O. 1965e. *A Modern English Grammar on Historical Principles.* Part V. London – Copenhagen: George Allen and Unwin LTD – Ejnar Munksgaad.
Jespersen, O. 1965f. *A Modern English Grammar on Historical Principles.* Part VI. London – Copenhagen: George Allen and Unwin LTD – Ejnar Munksgaad.
Jespersen, O. 1965g. *A Modern English Grammar on Historical Principles.* Part VII. London – Copenhagen: George Allen and Unwin LTD – Ejnar Munksgaad.
Jespersen, O. 1966. *Essentials of English Grammar.* London: George Allen and Unwin LTD.
Jespersen, O. 1972. *Growth and Structure of the English Language.* 9th ed. Oxford: Basil Blackwell Oxford.
Kjellmer, G. 1980. "There is No Hiding You in the House": On a Modal Use of the English Gerund. In: *English Studies,* 61:47 – 60.
Klégr, A. 1997. English Complex Prepositions of the Prepositional Phrase Type. In: *Acta Universitatis Carolinae – Philologica,* 5:51 – 78.
Kurzon, D. 1986. *It is hereby performed. Explorations in Legal Speech Acts.* Jerusalem: The Hebrew University of Jerusalem.
Kurzon, D. 1989. Language of the Law and Legal Language. In: *Special Language: From Humans Thinking to Thinking Machines.* Clevedon, Phil.: Multilingual Matters LTD.
Lees, R. B. 1960. *The Grammar of English Nominalizations.* The Hague: Mouton.
Leech, G. 1971. *Meaning and the English Verb.* London: Longman .
Leška, O., *et al.* (1977). *Princípy strukturní syntaxe II.* SPN: Praha.
Mair, Ch. 1988. Extraposed Gerundial Subject Clauses in Present-Day British English – An Investigation of the Corpus of the Survey of English Usage (University College of London). In: *Arbeiten aus Anglistik und Amerikanistik,* 13:51 – 63.
Maley, Y. 1987. The language of legislation. In: *Language in Society.* Vol. 16, No.1, Cambridge: CUP.

Maley, Y. 1994. The Language of the Law. In: *Language and the Law*. Longman: London and New York.
Marková, M. 1986. On the Relationship Between Gerund and Verbal Noun. In: *Philologica Pragensia,* 2:83 – 90.
Marchand, H. 1960. *The Categories and Types of Present-Day English Word-Formation. A Synchronic-Diachronic Approach.* Wiesbaden: Otto Harrassowitz.
Mathesius, V. 1913. O nominálních tendencích v slovesné predikaci novoanglické. In: *Sborník filologický,* 4:325 – 339.
Mathesius, V. 1966) *Řeč a sloh.* Praha: Československý spisovateľ.
Mathesius, V. 1975. *A Functional Analysis of Present-day English on a General Linguistic Basis.* Praha: SPN.
Mellinkoff, D. 1963. *The Language of the Law.* Boston: Little, Brown and Co.
Nižníková, J., Sokolová, M., a kol. (1998). *Valenčný slovník slovenských slovies.* Prešov: SLOVACONTACT, FF PU Prešov.
Nižníková, J. 1994. *Praktická príručka slovenskej skladby.* Prešov: SLOVACONTACT.
Nižníková, J. 2001. *Vetné modely v slovenčine.* Prešov: FF PU Prešov.
Nosek, J. 1954. Několik poznámek k polovětným vazbám v angličtine XVII. Století. *Acta Universitatis Carolinae,* 3:23 – 36.
Oravec,J., Bajzíková, E. 1982. *Súčasný slovenský spisovný jazyk – Syntax.* Bratislava: SPN.
Offences Against the Person Act 1861. London: Her Majesty's Stationary Office.
Oxford Dictionary of Law, Sixth edition. 2006. Oxford: OUP.
Oxford English Dictionary. 1989.
Quirk, R., et al. 1972. *A Grammar of Contemporary English.* London: Longman.
Quirk, R., *et al.* 1985. *A Comprehensive Grammar of the English Language* (CGEL), New York and London: Longman.
Quirk, R. 1995. *Grammatical and Lexical Variance in English.* London and New York: Longman.
Quirk, R., Greenbaum, S. 1996. *A Student's Grammar of the English Language.* London: Longman.
Rudanko, J. 1991. On verbs governing in *-ing* in present-day English. In: *English Studies,* 72:55 – 72.
Rudanko, J. 1992. *Resorting to* and *turning* to: On verbs governing to *-ing* in present-day English. In: *English Studies,* 73:68 – 79.
Rudanko, J. 1995. *Balking at* and *working at:* On verbs governing at *-ing* in present-day English. In: *English Studies,* 76:264 – 281.
Rudanko, J. 1996. *Prepositions and complement clauses.* State University of New York Press.

Sgall, P. 1993) Typy jazyku a jejich základní vlastnosti. In: *Slovo a slovesnost,* 54:271 – 277.

Strang, B.M.H. 1970. *A History of English*. London: Methuen and Co. LTD.

Štekauer, P. 2000. *Rudiments of the English Linguistics*. Prešov: SLOVA-CONTACT.

Štekauer, P. 1998. An Onomasiological Theory of English Word-Formation. *Studies in Functional and Structural Linguistics,* 46. Amsterdam/Philadelphia: John Benjamins Publishing Company.

Tesniere, L. 1934). Comment construire une syntaxe. Bulletin de la Faculté des Lettres de Strasbourg 12, pp. 219 – 229 in *Principy strukturní syntaxe II,* Praha: SPN, pp. 94 – 104.

Theft Act 1968. London: Her Majesty's Stationary Office.

Tomášek, M. 1998. *Překlad v právní praxi*. Praha: Linde Praha, a. s.

The Compact Oxford English Dictionary. 1991. Oxford: Clarendon Press.

The New Shorter Oxford English Dictionary. 1993. Oxford: Clarendon Press.

Trnka, B. 1956. *Rozbor nynější spisovné angličtiny III*. Praha: SPN.

Trosborg, A. (1991). An analysis of legal speech acts in English Contract Law. *Hermes, Journal of Linguistics* No.6. Copenhagen: CBS.

Trosborg, A., Bjarne B. (1992). An Analysis of Regulative Speech Acts in English Contracts. In: *Hermes, Journal of Linguistics* 9. Copenhagen: CBS.

Trosborg, A. (1992). The Performance of Legal discourse. In: *Hermes, Journal of Linguistics* 9. Copenhagen: CBS

Vachek, J. (1961). On Some Less Familiar Aspects of the Analytical Trend of English. In: *Brno Studies in English,* 3:9 – 44.

Vachek, J. (1972). *Historický vývoj angličtiny, 5. doplněné vydání*. Praha: SPN.

Vachek, J. (1990). *A Linguistic Characterology of Modern English*. Praha: SPN.

Vystrčilová, R. (2001). Jazyk práva. Stručný exkurz do problematiky překladu anglických a českých právních textu. In: *Časopis pro moderní filologii,* 1:1 – 10.

Webster's Third New International Dictionary of the English Language Unabridged. (1986). Springfield, Mass.

Wonder, J. P. (1970). Ambiguity and the English Gerund. In: *Lingua,* 3:254 – 267.

Peter Lang · Internationaler Verlag der Wissenschaften

Iwona Kokorniak

English *at*: An Integrated Semantic Analysis

Frankfurt am Main, Berlin, Bern, Bruxelles, New York, Oxford, Wien, 2007.
179 pp.
Polish Studies in English Language and Literature. Edited by Jacek Fisiak. Vol. 21
ISBN 978-3-631-57452-2 · pb. € 39.–*

This book aims to provide a considerably detailed, integrated and methodologically grounded study of *at* within the cognitive framework. Assuming the non-arbitrary quality of the mental lexicon and highly creative nature of the human conceptual system, it is posited that each preposition has a primary sense which interacts with a highly constrained set of cognitive principles to derive a set of additional distinct senses, forming a motivated semantic network. The present analysis also reveals that *at* is remarkably coherent in its metaphoric and metonymic manifestations in that there exists a high degree of family resemblances between all the uses discussed in this study. Theoretical investigation is set against empirical data to offer support for the claim that both native and advanced foreign language speakers appear to possess a high awareness and intuition about the proper conceptualization of individual *at*-senses.

Contents: Relations within categories · Identification of the primary sense and distinct senses of a preposition · The trajector-landmark configuration · The speaker-landmark correlation · Metaphoric and metonymic extensions · Polish prepositions · Conceptualization of *at* by native speakers

Frankfurt am Main · Berlin · Bern · Bruxelles · New York · Oxford · Wien
Distribution: Verlag Peter Lang AG
Moosstr. 1, CH-2542 Pieterlen
Telefax 0041 (0) 32 / 376 17 27

*The €-price includes German tax rate
Prices are subject to change without notice

Homepage http://www.peterlang.de